Our
LOVE JOURNEY

Our
LOVE JOURNEY

*The Story of a Modern Day
Aquila and Pricilla*

BARBARA J. WHITE

XULON PRESS

Xulon Press
2301 Lucien Way #415
Maitland, FL 32751
407.339.4217
www.xulonpress.com

© 2018 by Barbara J. White

All rights reserved solely by the author. The author guarantees all contents are original and do not infringe upon the legal rights of any other person or work. No part of this book may be reproduced in any form without the permission of the author. The views expressed in this book are not necessarily those of the publisher.

Unless otherwise indicated, Scripture quotations taken from the Amplified Bible (AMP). Copyright © 1954, 1958, 1962, 1964, 1965, 1987 by The Lockman Foundation. Used by permission. All rights reserved.

Scripture quotations taken from the King James Version (KJV)–*public domain.*

Printed in the United States of America.

ISBN-13: 9781545622964

Contents

Dedicated vii
Forward. ix
Preface xi

Chapter 1	Is this the End of Our Story?.	1
Chapter 2	The Green, Green Grass of Home . . . . Gordon's Roots – The Welsh Revival	10
Chapter 3	Early Childhood in Canada.	28
Chapter 4	Happy and Sad Times	47
Chapter 5	Adventurous Beginnings in England	63
Chapter 6	Revelations and Romance.	67
Chapter 7	Marriage and Ministry	75
Chapter 8	Crossing Over to the Other Side.	83
Chapter 9	Georgia: Soon On Our Mind.	88
Chapter 10	Pulling Up, Tearing Down, and Revival. . . .	96
Chapter 11	Launching Out Into the Deep	117
Chapter 12	Westward Bound – California Years	145
Chapter 13	Released to the Nations.	159
Chapter 14	Open Doors in Africa and Beyond	165
Chapter 15	Our First Ministry in Europe.	177
Chapter 16	Ministry in Pakistan and Kenya	187
Chapter 17	The Islands of the Sea.	202
Chapter 18	More Open Doors of Ministry in Europe . .	209
Chapter 19	South America is Calling	227
Chapter 20	Moving to the Country	232
Chapter 21	A New Millenium – A Change in Direction	254
Chapter 22	Down Under – Another Dream Comes True.	265
Chapter 23	The Now Season of My Life.	269
Addendum	Three Years Later	277

Dedication

Dedicated to the Aquila and Pricilla's of this generation, the husband and wife teams who are called to minister in the anointing and fire of the Holy Spirit, God confirming His Word with mighty signs and wonders.

> Great is the Lord, and highly to be praised, and His greatness is unsearchable. One generation shall praise Your works to another, and shall declare Your Mighty acts.
>
> −Psalm 145:3-4 NASB

Foreword

We have known Gordon and Barbara White for nearly forty years and we can say that *Our Love Journey* from Barbara's hand is more than just a glimpse into the lives of a modern day Aquila and Priscilla.

Though Gordon is now with the Father, the life and love he and Barbara shared for many years as they traveled the globe touching thousands of lives for Jesus Christ lives on in the beautiful testimonies of this inspiring autobiography.

Personally, the influence Gordon and Barbara have had on our lives over the years we have known them, traveled with them, and ministered with them, served greatly to strengthen Nancy and me, impacting our ministry in myriad ways. Two of our closest and dearest friends, Gordon and Barbara have spoken many confirming words by the Spirit of God into our lives that have come to pass and are still coming to pass.

Gordon and Barbara, this "Aquila and Priscilla", were exemplary in daily intercessory prayer as a couple, even during times when Gordon was ill. They faithfully preached the Word of His Grace and Faith, exhorted the Body of Christ to keep their cares cast on the Lord, and powerfully flowed in the gifts of tongues and interpretation of tongues throughout their many years of ministry. Together they demonstrated a uniqueness and openness in following the Holy Spirit from which Nancy and I, our church, and the Body of Christ worldwide greatly benefitted.

As you read Gordon and Barbara's love story and the powerful, and at times humorous testimonies throughout this book, allow yourselves to be blessed, encouraged, inspired, and impacted by the Love of Jesus that practically leaps from these pages. Thanks, Barbara, for sharing and enriching our lives! Even so, as Gordon always exclaimed, "If God be for us – *case closed*!"

Pastors Paul and Nancy Glass
– Rex World Outreach, Rex, Georgia

Preface

The blazing sunsets quickly disappear over the California skies. One moment, the brilliant orange, red and yellow hues – sometimes mingled with a hint of blue and pink – are shining brilliantly in the western evening sky, and the next moment they quickly disappear into the distant Pacific Ocean.

As I write, I reflect on a recent sunset in my life. How quickly our lives are lived, they pass before us, and suddenly a major change. The one you loved so dearly for over fifty years is gone. Not forever; it is a temporary separation, yet so painful at times. I know in my heart we shall be united again in heaven and for eternity.

Yet, before there can be a sunset, there must be a sunrise. A sunrise always begins in the east. This is God's order. I remember the sunrise in my life that brought such an awareness of God's incredible plan for my life. His plan evolved as I took a few bold steps to position myself for the future. So young, perhaps naive in many ways, but I had a fearless boldness and desire to please the One who had called me to serve Him. As a child, I knew His call on my life. Missionary, pastor's wife, or, "what Lord do you want me to do?" The myriads of memories that flash before me give me immense comfort.

I know my sunrise was planned in love by my Heavenly Father. He planned carefully ahead of time for me, and I prayerfully took paths that would bring me to His purpose for my life here on the earth.

Our love story is amazing. It is matchless and completely unique because of the Father's love and plan for Gordon and me. Only He could take a young Canadian girl from the east coast of Canada, affected by insecurities from a broken home, and match her with a young man from South Wales. We were born into different cultures, family backgrounds, and upbringings. I experienced little hope for my future as a teenager because of the divorce of my parents. The vision for my future was so dim at times, but I held on to the word God gave me when I was twelve years old.

On the other hand, Gordon grew up in the valleys of South Wales where coal mining was the predominant occupation. It was a dreary life surrounded by hardship and small incomes. Fear gripped him as a young child and opened the door to stuttering. How could God use him to preach His Word with this impediment?

Gordon survived the ravages of World War II in London, England. Hope waned as he grew into manhood. He served in the Royal Air Force and pursued different occupations, but none brought fulfillment until he heard God's call and followed His plan. Gordon's godly and praying maternal grandmother Pritchard, who was involved in the great Welsh Revival of 1904/1905 affected his life. I believe her prayers marked him for the calling that rested on his life.

How could our paths cross? Who could arrange such a marriage? How in the world could a young woman in the western hemisphere meet this handsome, dark haired young man thousands of miles to the east, separated by the Atlantic Ocean? Only our Heavenly Father could initiate and bring together such a union. We had one important factor in common – we both loved the Lord and were committed to do His will.

This is our love story, a beautiful journey we shared for fifty years. It was our desire to chronicle this journey, so I began writing a few years ago. We both felt we should share the mighty work and ministry God wrought through His grace and gifting upon our lives. Our ministry was a husband and wife team, like that of Aquila and Pricilla in the New Testament. It began with assisting other men of God, then serving in pastoral ministry, and on to preaching in the nations. So many were transformed and healed through the power of God.

I had no idea my Aquila would not be here for the continued writing and publication of our book. I have written Gordon's chapters on his behalf. I know he would be pleased that our story is available to inspire others, especially couples, to be obedient to the plan of God for their lives. Through

God's grace the ministry continues. My desire is to arouse others to seek the Lord Jesus with all their heart and follow Him. He truly has an incredible, specific plan for each life.

Our Heavenly Father's promise to each of us: "I will instruct you and teach you in the way which you should go; I will counsel you with My eye upon you" (Psalm 32:8 NASB).

Our story is His story for it is a work of the Holy Spirit and to God be all the praise and glory! What bonded us together for fifty years? Read on and be inspired by this exciting journal of God's grace.

–Barbara J. White

Chapter 1

Is This The End of Our Story?

My eyes fell on the familiar red cover of the New Testament on the kitchen counter. *The Translator's New Testament* became a favorite for Gordon to read each day. He loved to read to me each evening before we had our time of prayer. It was a special time together.

I picked up the New Testament and browsed through the pages, especially taking note of the personal scribbles he had tucked between the pages on various types of paper. "Hmm", I mused as I picked up a small note. It caught my eye.

"Did Gordon leave this message for me to read at this time?" Our fiftieth wedding Anniversary was approaching, and it was not going to be easy when the date arrived.

> What is there in the vale of life,
> Half so delightful as a wife,
> When friendship, love and peace combine,
> It stamps the marriage bond divine.
> –William Cowper

The moment was emotionally overwhelming as I read the poem. Somehow in my heart I knew he left it there for me to read. The timing was precise and the moment is etched on my heart. The joy that rose in my heart took precedence over the recent sadness. Oh, how Gordon loved me – and how I loved him! We did not make it to our fiftieth wedding anniversary on August 19, but all that matters is that we made it to the day of his graduation to heaven on June 26, 2014.

What were the events that led up to Gordon's promotion? It was a day to day journey over the past three years. One of the ministries of the Holy Spirit is to show us things to come (John 16:13). This is exactly what the Holy Spirit did to prepare me for this moment in time. I knew in my heart he would be going to heaven, not exactly when, but I knew it would not be delayed for too long.

Was it easy? Not at all – at times extremely distressing on the mind, emotions, and flesh. But the Lord faithfully equipped me to face the challenges that would come so that I could meet them in faith and victory. The Holy Spirit never reveals information without working in your spirit, building strength and comfort. I made a commitment to walk through this season in the love of God. Negative feelings and thoughts would rise, but I had a choice and He helped me to stay the course.

I had dreams of our latter years whereby we would enjoy time to relax after fifty years of pastoral and international ministry travelling to many nations. Maybe we would enjoy vacations or a road trip, even day trips to the beach or desert. It was not to be. I began walking down a road I had never walked before. Each day the Lord was preparing me for the future and His grace was carrying me along. Daily He stretched me and showed me I had "strength for all things in Christ Who empowers me ... Who infuses inner strength into me; I am self sufficient in Christ's sufficiency." (Philippians 4:13 AMP).

The weeks leading up to his graduation were challenging as his body was declining. He clung to the Word of God and stayed in faith right up to the time of his departure. In the latter weeks, the Lord taught me to lower my expectations of improvement. I knew Gordon was on his way to heaven.

His diminished health had begun a few years earlier with various ailments. In 2002, Gordon had a heart attack, necessitating a four-way bypass surgery, from which he quickly recovered. A new lease on life enabled him to travel for a few years to minister in Europe, Australia, and the United States.

Gordon developed a growing abdominal aortic aneurysm, which could have ruptured and taken his life at any moment. Thank God this did not occur. The condition COPD (chronic obstructive pulmonary disease) gradually caused shortness of breath, necessitating the use of oxygen. Sometimes his oxygen level dropped to seventy two percent, a dangerous level indeed. The sad story is he was reluctant to use oxygen twenty-four hours a day, especially when leaving the house. The years of hypertension had taken a toll as well. Other issues were a thyroid goiter and coronary artery disease. His body was simply worn out.

One month before my husband went to be with the Lord, he was treated in the hospital's ICU with further tests and an MRI. The doctor concluded that his vital organs were compressed as a result of osteoporosis and he would need to be in hospice care at home.

Each caregiver who ministered to him in our home was treated with such love. His concern was what he could do for them. "Is there anything you want me to pray for?", he would often ask. His sweet smile and humor were amazing to all who came to see him.

I made a few opportunities to talk to him about going to heaven. "Do you think, sweetie, that you have finished your course and completed all God called you to do? I can hear the Lord saying to you, 'Well done thou good and faithful servant.'" He was not ready to go at that time. His concern was always, "What about you, Barbara, what are you going to do?" I always assured him that the Lord would look after me, and I would carry on with the ministry.

Gordon was an exceptionally caring husband and loved me deeply. He was a loving father to our three children, Jason (Michelle) White, Russell White, and Zoe (Perry) Parris, and the most adored Papa by our seven grandchildren. Zara, Seth, Alexa, Nathan, Kate, Alex, and Luke loved him and cherished the many precious memories and fun times they had together. Gordon had an amazing smile and British sense of humor.

During January 2014, he was concerned that I find the piano I had been praying for. He took the initiative and found contact numbers from the local newspaper. When I phoned the last number, the business man who answered said, "I have the piano you are looking for." Sure enough, when we went to see it the next day, it looked like new. Gordon bought it for me that day. I treasure his last gift to me. Each time I play and worship the Lord, my heart pours out love to my Savior. It has become an instrument of healing as I process my loss.

I honor the life and rich spiritual legacy that Gordon left his family. He had such a love for God's Word and the anointing of the Holy Spirit. His strong faith kept him during these last months. He was a unique man who had a passion for seeing men and women come to the knowledge of Jesus as Savior, Lord, Healer, and Deliverer. His passion and love for Jesus never waned. He was truly a man after God's own heart, filled with compassion for the lost and suffering. He would take time to talk to the homeless and distressed, share Jesus with them, and often gave them money for a meal.

As a family we were blessed to celebrate Gordon's eighty-second birthday on May 25. When Father's Day arrived on June 15 we again celebrated together at home. Gordon never liked to make much of birthdays or special days, but I know he enjoyed all the attention from the children and grandchildren.

Gordon's time of graduation was coming closer each day. On June 25 he was quite alert and talked continuously. The following day there was a change.

"Barbara", his sweet voice called me to his bedside, "Am I really going to heaven soon?", he asked. With an excitement in my spirit, reflected in my voice, and tears flowing down my face as I held his hand I said, "Yes, honey, you are going to heaven soon. Jesus is waiting for you. You are going to see Him very soon." With a twinkle in his eyes he responded with these words, "Barbara, you wouldn't be kidding me would you?" His British humor was still alive.

"Oh no sweetie, I would never kid you about this", was my reply. With tears streaming down my face I knew his time of departure was at hand. He had a glimpse into the glory realm and was ready to go. His last precious words are indelibly imprinted on my heart and cause me to smile every time I recall them. They are so uniquely Gordon.

He fell into a deep, peaceful sleep and within two hours, at 5:10 p.m. on June 26 he left the earth realm to enter into the fullness of the joy of heaven. I sat with him, along with my son-in-law, Perry, and Gordon's precious caregiver, Chanel. We witnessed the most beautiful moment, aware of how holy and glorious it is to be with the Lord. Because of Jesus, to die is gain and death had lost its sting. The glory of the Lord was incredibly present at that moment.

I honor you dear Gordon. You fought a good fight, you finished your course, you kept the faith (2 Timothy 4:7). One of Gordon's favorite quotes from Romans 8:31 is affectionately remembered by those who knew him. I felt led to have it imprinted on his gravestone.

Since God is for us – Case Closed!

My Tribute To My Dear Gordon

From the little coal mining town of Argoed, South Wales you came,
With a call of God on your life, but you never wanted to make a name,
Preserved during the bombings of World War II
It soon became evident that God had His hand on you.

It wasn't the Royal Air Force or a civil service job for you
God lifted you up and called you to go –
nations were waiting
To hear the Good News, the Gospel of Grace,
You were soon to begin your ministry and run your race.

Not alone, it was not to be! For two are better than one don't you see,
You had a divine appointment in London one day:
A young red haired girl walked into your life,
An answer to your prayer – it really was love at first sight!

Our Love Journey

Fifty years since the day I said, "I do",
have brought multiplied blessings:
Two sons and a daughter, seven grandchildren, too.
You called me your Pricilla, your partner in ministry,
Together we labored here and in lands across the sea.

You loved me deeply, but greater love was for your Lord
As you toiled with a passion for the lost and hurting,
You so graciously paused to speak an encouraging word,
to rich or to poor,
Great rewards were waiting as you stepped through the door.

Forever loving you! Barbara

Our Pastor, Mike Webb at Foothill Family Church in Lake Forest, California, conducted a beautiful memorial service on July 9, 2014, at the graveside in Riverside, California. We were surrounded by my family from Canada and so many of our precious friends from Foothill Family Church. Ministers and associate ministers came from Georgia and San Francisco. Our son Jason gave a beautiful eulogy honoring the life of his Dad, sharing special humorous moments. Zara, our oldest granddaughter, brought an emotionally moving message in honor of her beloved Papa. The pall bearers were sons, Jason and Russell, son-in-law Perry, my brothers Audley and Elden, and grandson Nathan.

Is this the end of our story? In the light of eternity, it could be likened to the end of a paragraph.

Now to the beginning. Our love story began many years ago.

Chapter 2

The Green, Green Grass of Home
Gordon's Roots – The Welsh Revival

My entrance into the world was on a Wednesday, May 25, 1932, at our home called *Fairoak,* in Argoed, Monmouthshire which was situated in the *cwm* (small valley). Argoed, nestled in the Rhymny Valley is located just north of Cardiff in South Wales, Great Britain.

Cymru is the Welsh name for Wales. Welsh identity emerged among the Celtic Britons after the Roman withdrawal from Britain in the fifth century. Wales is regarded as one of the modern Celtic nations (Wikipedia). The Welsh language evolved from the Celtic language spoken by the ancient Britons. Roots of this language are connected to Gaul and Briton in France. Today approximately twenty percent of the people in Wales speak Welsh. To preserve the language all Welsh children study Welsh in school up to sixteen years of age.

Wales is known as the *Land of Song*, famous for its Welsh Male Voice Choirs. The melodious stringed instrument, the harp, is the national musical instrument and is still being manufactured by hand with skilled craftsmen. It can take one year for one harp to be finished.

I am the youngest of four children born to William Stanley White and Edith Barlow (nee Pritchard) White. My siblings are Pearl, Glynn, and June. I am named after my Uncle (Bob) Robert Pritchard and Uncle Gordon White.

When Grancha (Welsh for grandfather) William Barlow Pritchard married Gran Elizabeth Griffiths (Gruffydd in Welsh) Pritchard, they lived in the historic slate mining town of Blawnau Ffestiniog in North Wales. It is known as the "town that roofed the world." The village is close to Snowdonia Mountain, the highest mountain in Wales. Today it is a tourist center for those trekking and hiking the rugged mountain. My grandparents joined the movement to south Wales during the slump in slate quarrying when the coal mines of the south were burgeoning. Argoed is surrounded by green mountains today, but when I was born, active coal mines had turned the hillsides into dark slag heaps.

I have been told my father's family originated in Scotland. Other family members have mentioned the Whites were of Jewish or Spanish descent as many Jews migrated from Europe and settled in Wales. If Jewish, this accounts for the business acumen of the Whites. They owned businesses and hotels in Wales and Hampton Hill, near London. The Roebuck Hotel in Hampton Hill, once owned by my Aunt Lily, was a lodging for Clark Gable during World War II.

My father worked as an engine driver in one of the local coal mines while we lived in South Wales. My paternal grandmother, Ellen White, was widowed sometime before 1911. She owned a grocery store connected to their home, *Bryn Gwyn*, in Aberbargoed, Monmouthshire.

My early years were spent in Argoed playing on the mountains around our home. I enjoyed a simple childhood. Twice I cut my wrist on broken glass as I played on the sides of the mountains and was rushed to the doctor. On one occasion God used a Japanese doctor to save my life. Looking back I see how God's hand was on me. Satan could have easily snuffed out my young life, but God had a plan; I believe my godly Gran Pritchard kept me in her prayers.

Each birthday the words of a Welsh ditty were spoken over me by my Mam (Mother in Welsh), "Libby lobby lay, it's your birthday today," followed by tender pulls on my hair corresponding to my age. I have passed this Welsh tradition down, speaking the same words over my children and grandchildren on their birthdays.

On Friday nights we were taken to the neighboring town of Blackwood on the bus to shop with my Mam. We always came home with groceries, including thick double cream lavishly poured over bananas. This was a special treat; rich British cream has always been a favorite in my diet.

On Sunday afternoons I have memories of walks with my Dad and Mam, followed by teatime. My Mam made the best apple and blackberry tart, again served with thick cream. Welsh cakes were her specialty and we have followed the tradition of Welsh cakes in our home.

A treat we looked forward to was a yearly trip on the *charabanc* (open-top sightseeing bus) to the beach at Barry Island near Cardiff on the Bristol Channel. Along with all the other families from the mining valleys, this was our annual summer holiday.

As a young lad, along with my friends, I picked up cigarette ends and smoked them. My concerned Mam, wanting to break me of this shameful habit, thought she would teach me a lesson. She called the local constable (*bobby*), and asked him to visit our home with a stern warning directed toward me, alarming me of the consequences of this habit. The incident opened the door to fear to such a degree that I began stuttering. My Mam meant well, and I am sure she would not have done this if she had known the end result.

I was seven years old when World War II started. We must have been living in London then because I remember one night the corner of our house in Hampton Hill was hit by a bomb. On another occasion during the war we were about to leave the home of my maternal Gran, Elizabeth Pritchard, when I started screaming and refused to leave the house. Since I was determined not to leave with them, my family remained in Gran's house. Just a few minutes later a bomb landed on the street. If we had left we could have all been killed. God gave me a sense of foreboding that something dangerous was about to happen. The spirit of a child can be keenly sensitive to the voice of the Lord. I thank Him for giving me a warning not to go out into the street. I have been told my Gran never went into the air-raid shelters during the war; her trust was fully in the Lord for protection.

Sometime during the war we were evacuated back to South Wales, but while in London dark black-out curtains were drawn each night in the houses so that they could not be detected by the "buzzbombs" released by the German planes. "The Blitz", with its nightly bombings terrified me. This quite likely added to my stuttering problem as a child and into my youth. It was not until I was born again that stuttering left and I was free of this impediment.

At the end of the war many members of our extended family moved from Wales back to Camberwell in south-east London. While there, I attended nearby Peckham Grammar School. Later we moved to a house in East Molesey, Surrey, where I lived with my parents during my single years.

The heritage of my faith was passed down to me from my Gran Pritchard. I remember hearing of an experience she had when she was young, alone in her bedroom. She had a strong desire to pray and so dropped to her knees. With arms in the air, these words came out of her mouth, "My Lord and my God", and she felt as if her body was on fire. Gran had a vision before the Welsh Revival came, and another one before the First World War. The Welsh Revival broke out on October 31, 1904, at Moriah Chapel in Loughor, Wales. She was involved in this revival which lasted from 1904-1905 during Evan Roberts' era. Many women were involved in the revival as documented in the book, *Carriers of The Fire* by Karen Lowe. Gran had a prophetic anointing foreseeing men being carried up by angels to heaven as a result of many deaths and great destruction during the First World War.

During my childhood years in Wales I was taken by my Mam to the little Baptist Chapel in Argoed, but I never really heard the salvation message. Mam would often tell me, "Gordon, when you grow up, ask God to make you healthy, wealthy, and wise." She didn't understand what she was saying, but those words stayed with me. After I got saved, I realized this is really the Gospel: to be a whole person, healthy and having all your needs abundantly met. This was confirmed as I later read, "Beloved, I wish above all things that thou mayest prosper and be in health, even as thy soul prospereth." (3 John 2).

There was a certain amount of religious legalism involved in the Welsh chapels: "Never use the scissors on a Sunday; do not read the Sunday newspaper", among other religious rules. However, my Uncle Bob would buy the Sunday newspaper, save it and read it on Monday. This legalism included not being allowed to play on Sunday. Everyone went to chapel and an air of melancholy lay over the land that day.

I served two years of military duty in the Royal Air Force in the early 1950's and was stationed in Whittering, England, and in Aberdeenshire, Scotland, near Balmoral Castle. Upon completion of my military duty, I went to work for the British Civil Service in the Inland Revenue. I also applied to be a finger print technician in Scotland Yard but was not accepted. I sought work as an engine driver on British Rail, but that door closed as well. The Lord had another plan for my life.

Soccer was an important part of my young adult life and I played for local teams for many years. I tried out for the larger Wimbledon team but was not accepted; this was not God's plan for me, either. One time I was asked to be the goalie for my local team as they competed against the Clapham Common team. It was a disaster – I let twenty-three balls into the net. Never again was I asked to play that position. I loved to run and won awards for the one hundred yard dash. My ability to run fast was contrary to what the doctors told my parents after I had rheumatic fever as a child. "Gordon will never be able to run," they said, but the Lord healed my heart.

Tongues Are For a Sign

As a young man I searched for truth but looked in the wrong places. I thought it was found in intellectualism and spent time reading the great writers. My search also took me to the nightclubs and horse race gambling.

This lifestyle brought no peace or satisfaction to my heart. One Sunday night my Aunt Mary, an older sister of my Mam, a godly woman, invited me to go to church with her. Since I was bored and had nothing better to do I decided to accompany her to the local Pentecostal church in Hounslow, near London airport. It was a small insignificant building with a corrugated tin roof, what you might say was located "on the other side of the tracks." I found a seat near the back of the church and decided to sit it out. Everyone was singing and clapping their hands, and they seemed happy enough. During the service a little lady got up and spoke in a language that sounded like Arabic. I was stunned. I knew this lady, she had little education and could hardly speak the Queen's English, let alone a foreign language. This lady was my Aunt Mary!

She was speaking fluently in a language I did not understand, it was beyond my intellectual comprehension. The preacher gave the interpretation of the message in tongues, but that didn't impress me as much as the speaking in tongues by this little lady that I knew so well. I was arrested by the power of God. The Holy Spirit convinced me God was much closer and more real than I had thought. At the end of the service I went forward and asked the pastor to pray with me to receive Jesus. That Sunday night in 1953 I accepted Jesus as my Lord and Savior. The transforming power of the Gospel began to affect my life, and I became a new creation in Christ Jesus.

Later on I read in 1 Corinthians 14: 22 that "tongues are for a sign, not to them that believe, but to them that believe not…" The Amplified Bible states it this way: *"Thus [unknown] tongues are meant for a [supernatural] sign, not for believers but for unbelievers [on the point of believing]."*

One of the habits that stayed with me for awhile was smoking. In the 1950's, there was no link to cancer or other adverse health effects from smoking. No one told me I should not smoke because my body was now a temple of the Holy Spirit (1 Corinthians 6:19). However, the Holy Spirit brought conviction to my heart. I was witnessing to a friend about the Lord in a café in London as I puffed on my cigarette. I probably offered him one, too. As I told him how the Lord could deliver him from sin and all bondages in his life, the Holy Spirit convinced me that I needed to be set free from my own bondage of nicotine. I made a commitment to gradually stop and set a time when I would not smoke again. Praise God, the Lord delivered me.

After I was born again, I attended the local Elim Pentecostal Church in Kingston-upon-Thames, Surrey, situated close to where I lived with my parents in East Molesey. The famous

Hampton Court Palace, King Henry VIII's former residence, is only a short distance away on the River Thames. This palace is one of the three locations where Bible scholars translated the King James Version of our Bible in 1611.

God used the local Elim Pentecostal church to disciple me in the fundamental truths of the Christian life. I took opportunities to serve the Lord in nursing home outreaches and taught Sunday school at the local Church of England on Sunday afternoons. Seeking the baptism in the Holy Spirit became essential in my walk with the Lord. It was a struggle; and I kept thinking God was going to do the speaking, so I kept waiting for Him to do something. For two years, I sought to receive this wonderful gift but never understood how to receive until the day I attended a meeting where the Canadian evangelist Lorne Fox was ministering. Once again, I went forward to be prayed for to receive the baptism in the Holy Spirit. Suddenly I had the revelation that I needed to speak in this new language, so I stepped out in faith and began to speak a word or two. It then flowed out of my spirit like rivers of living water that Jesus spoke of in John 7:37- 39:

> "In the last day, that great day of the feast, Jesus stood and cried saying, If any man thirst, let him come unto me and drink. He that believeth on me, as the scripture hath said, out of his belly shall flow rivers of living water." (John 7:37-39)

During this time my mode of transportation was a bicycle; I used it to go to and from work and attend church. I had been given books written by Evangelist T.L. Osborne and Rev. Kenneth E. Hagin and learned from their writing and the Scriptures that I could believe God to provide for my needs and desires according to Mark 11:22-24. Jesus said:

> "Have faith in God. For verily I say unto you, That whosoever shall say unto this mountain, Be thou removed and be thou cast into the sea; and shall not doubt in his heart, but shall believe that those things which he saith shall come to pass: he shall have whatsoever he saith. Therefore I say unto you, What things so-ever ye desire, when ye pray, believe that ye receive them, and ye shall have them."

Since I needed a car, I made a decision to ask God to provide a car, and I believed I received it according to what Jesus said in these Scriptures. I had no idea how God was going to do it, or when it would come to pass. I continued to believe God's Word. I dared to ask the Lord to put the car outside my house.

I told Mam about this prayer request and she responded with the words, "But Gordon, you will need to save your money so that you can buy one." I just kept on believing, but did not share my prayer request with anyone else.

One day, maybe nine months later, as I came home from work and turned the corner into our street on my old bicycle, I saw a shiny black Wolesley automobile with running boards, sitting outside our house. I wondered who was visiting my parents. As soon as I entered the house, Mam excitedly announced to me that the car was mine.

"You mean that car really belongs to me?" I questioned.

"Yes, Gordon, it is your car. One of our neighbors decided to give it to you!"

My only contact with these people was the occasional polite exchanges when I met them on the street. I was stunned. How did this happen? What caused them to make such a decision?

I realized it was God. This was the answer to my prayer of faith. It was parked right outside my front door. My faith was well developed in believing for the car, but I had not learned to drive. It didn't take me long to get the driving lessons started, and soon I was a qualified British driver.

In December 1962, as I was reading the local newspaper, my eyes were drawn to an advertisement for Full Gospel meetings to be held in London. I dialed the local phone number and found out the person was Rev. Selwyn Hughes. He lived locally in my home town of East Molesey, Surrey. I soon connected with Selwyn and accompanied him to the meetings he was sponsoring.

The January 1963 meetings were held in the Metropolitan Tabernacle, also identified as Spurgeon's Tabernacle, in the southeast district of London known as the Elephant and Castle. The guest speaker was Rev. A.C. Valdez Jr. of Milwaukee, Wisconsin. I had the privilege of assisting Selwyn in these meetings, which were held during the coldest winter in England for many years. In spite of freezing temperatures and snow storms the people came. The power of God was manifested as Rev. Valdez allowed the Holy Spirit and His gifts to flow through him with resulting healings, miracles, salvation, and the baptism of the Holy Spirit.

He also spoke on the subject of Bible prosperity—how God wanted to bless His people financially. He prayed over small cloths, called *prosperity cloths*, and distributed them to those who desired to prosper. This was all well and good, but we lacked sound Bible teaching on the subject. It caused me to search the Scriptures on this vital Bible subject, and little by little the Holy Spirit revealed the correct Bible truth to my spirit. My mind began to be renewed.

Following the meetings at Spurgeon's Tabernacle, Selwyn started the London Revival Crusade, and held weekly Sunday afternoon meetings at Dennison House, near Victoria Station. I continued to assist him. I enjoyed the ministry of a fellow Welshman whose preaching delivery held my and the congregation's attention with his articulate command of the English language. The Spirit of God moved in a refreshing way with the utterance gifts of the Holy Spirit manifesting on a regular basis. There was an excitement as people of different denominations came to receive more, and many were baptized in the Holy Spirit. Soon mid-week services were started on Friday nights. Selwyn would bring in well known guest speakers, such as Gordon Lindsay of Christ For The Nations of Dallas, Texas, and T.L Osborne from Tulsa, Oklahoma.

The second of these evangelistic meetings where I assisted Selwyn was in July of 1963 in a tent erected on an old bomb site near the Elephant and Castle. Rev. Morris Cerullo of San Diego was the guest evangelist. Again, many were saved, healed and baptized in the Holy Spirit. It was the first time I witnessed large numbers of people baptized in the Holy Spirit all at the same time. Brother Morris asked me to join him in praying for the people.

During August of that year, I accompanied Selwyn and many of the people who attended the London Revival Crusade to Oral Roberts' first healing crusade in the United Kingdom, which was held in the city of Newport, South Wales.

I continued to faithfully serve and help Selwyn and regularly sang solos in the meetings. When Selwyn organized an evangelistic meeting in the Royal Albert Hall, he asked me to minister in song. I was also asked to preach and sing at an evangelistic outreach in Trafalgar Square in May of 1964.

I was now in my early thirties, and I knew it was time to get serious about believing the Lord for a wife. I prayed and watched from the platform, observing every young lady who came to the meetings.

During the later part of the summer of 1963, a remarkable and most unexpected event occurred in my life. During one of the mid-week meetings I made an unusual request to the Lord. I observed a young, red haired woman attending the meetings on a regular basis. I had never spoken to her so I knew nothing of her background, spiritual life, or even where she came from. I asked the Lord, "Is she the one?"

More Signs

I do not advocate *making fleeces* when it comes to receiving direction from the Lord, as one can get fleeced. New Testament believers are to be led by the Spirit of the Lord and receive the witness in their own spirit as to being guided correctly. However, I made a request to the Lord that turned out to be quite supernatural, and God met me right where I was in my spiritual understanding.

During this mid-week meeting some in the service were being used in the utterance gifts of the Holy Spirit (tongues, interpretation of tongues, and prophecy). Just prior to thi‚s I asked the Lord to give me a sign concerning this young lady whom I had been watching with interest.

I said, "Lord, use her in the gift of tongues tonight." I wanted a divine indication that I was being directed to develop a relationship with her. I prayed this prayer just between me and the Lord. No one else was aware of my request, not even the devil knew of my desire. I didn't have to wait long for my answer. Soon this young woman stood to her feet, uttered a message in tongues, and Selwyn Hughes interpreted it. To the congregation it was not unusual for someone to give a message in tongues, but it was important to me, a sign that perhaps God was drawing me to her. What I was to learn later was that Barbara, although baptized in the Holy Spirit from the age of fourteen, had never given a public message in tongues in church. This was the first occasion. She certainly was not aware that I had prayed this prayer – it was truly supernatural.

Barbara's Account of This Unusual Sign From the Lord:

I had been experiencing great blessings from attending the London Revival Crusade. There was an excitement in my spirit and an anticipation that good things were happening. My hunger for the Lord was increasing, and on this particular evening I sensed the presence of the Holy Spirit in a new way. As one or two others were being used in the utterance gifts of the Holy Spirit, I suddenly felt enveloped with the power of the Holy Spirit. It was a fresh experience, intense with a great pressure on my chest, accompanied with my heart beating faster and faster. "What is happening?" I thought. "What am I supposed to do?"

As soon as these questions surfaced in my mind, Selwyn Hughes spoke out a supernatural word of knowledge. I took note of what he was saying – I felt desperate to know what to do in this strange situation. The word he spoke went right into my spirit, "There is a person here tonight whom God wants to use in the gift of tongues for the first time." I knew this word was for me.

With great fear and trepidation, I stood to my feet and spoke the tongue the Lord gave me; then trembling, I quickly sat down. I do not remember the interpretation of the tongue that Selwyn gave. All I knew I was extremely relieved that I had obeyed the Lord. I felt quite overcome by the experience. I had never specifically asked the Lord to use me in this way, although I had been drawing closer to Him and seeking His face over the recent months.

It would be a few weeks before I would learn of Gordon's prayer on that unforgettable night. The end of August 1963 was approaching. Up to this time, Gordon and I had not conversed with each another. It was a beautiful warm summer evening. At the close of the Friday evening meeting my friend Marion Hall (nee Clarke) unexpectedly introduced me to Gordon. She had known him from various youth meetings in other churches. I later realized this was the key to carrying on a conversation. Proper British protocol required that Gordon be formally introduced to me. So down came the cultural wall, and we began to talk briefly after the service. Marion and I planned to go on a week's holiday down in Cornwall. As we discussed our plans Gordon sweetly interrupted and asked me to send him a postcard.

"Sure, I would be glad to," I responded," but I don't have your address." It didn't take long for Gordon to produce his address, and we said our goodbyes.

As much as I enjoyed my holiday with Marion in Cornwall, my thoughts were back in London. I was greatly looking forward to seeing Gordon again. "Would he pursue a relationship? Or, perhaps he will ask me out to tea after church on Sunday afternoon?" were some of the questions I pondered during that week.

Chapter 3

Early Childhood in Canada

The rush hour traffic was building up on the 15 Freeway as we headed north from Corona, California, towards the 60 Freeway on-ramp on our way to Los Angeles. Although our meeting was scheduled for 7 p.m., we allowed plenty of time to make our way through the endless lines of commuters whizzing westward, homeward bound.

"We'll soon be able to get in the car pool lane", I commented. I was driving so that Gordon could rest and meditate on the message he would be preaching that evening. No sooner had I pulled over into the car pool lane on the 60 Freeway when I suddenly had a flash back to my early years growing up in Canada.

I chuckled as I said to Gordon, "When I was a child or teenager I never dreamed I would be driving all over the Los Angeles freeways, much less driving with my husband to minister at a well-known Los Angeles church."

Sometimes in jest Gordon, would remind me,"If you hadn't met me you would be packing sardines in a New Brunswick cannery!"

I would retort, "Oh that was never *my* dream!"

Then I would tease Gordon, "If you hadn't met me, you would be working in the coal mines of South Wales."

We enjoyed ribbing each other about our roots with very differing backgrounds.

It was a Wednesday, June 12, 1940, when I made my entrance into the world in the McClellan Memorial Hospital, a small rural hospital in Riverside, Albert County, New Brunswick, Canada. I was the second child born to my parents, George and Beulah Newcomb, but I am the eldest living child, as my older sister Shirley was stillborn. My parents took me home to live in the neighboring community of Hopewell Hill. This small hamlet overlooks the expansive marshland that eventually ends at the tidal Peticodiac River.

It was a simple country life surrounded by my father's relatives, including many cousins. Growing up everyone called me Barbara Jean. From birth, I was dedicated to the Lord and was taken to the small Hopewell Hill Pentecostal church located near the top of the hill. The one room church with hard wooden benches seemed insignificant next to the more stately Baptist and Methodist churches located in succession on the hill.

In her early twenties my Mother moved to Hopewell Hill from Halifax, Nova Scotia to help the lady pastor, Miss Hubley, pioneer the Pentecostal message in that area. Mom was the red-headed, lady evangelist who not only preached, but played the piano and sang. I recall her stories of walking many miles to and from the meetings in the surrounding villages. Among her converts, she had led my father, George Edgar Newcomb, to the Lord in those revival meetings. His parents had divorced and he had been brought up by his grandparents and aunts. He worked for the local lumber mill owned by his grandfather, George Whitfield Newcomb.

On May 19, 1937, a year after my Father's conversion, my parents were married in the Full Gospel Church in Halifax and began their married life in Hopewell Hill. Dad built a little home for the family on land given to him by his grandfather. Our family calls it the *Little Green House That Grew*, because a few years later it was enlarged by raising the roof and creating an upstairs with three bedrooms and an inside bathroom. By the time I was four, my sister Elizabeth Ruth, whom we call Betty, arrived on the scene. In fun we say, "Betty raised the roof."

When I was quite young, my father enlisted in the Royal Canadian Air Force, and we lived for a short time in Toronto and Godrich, Ontario.

During 1945, at the end of World War II, we moved to Halifax where Dad worked for the owner of an engineering firm in the shipyards of Halifax Harbor. We lived in the basement apartment of the large home of Harris and Sadie Webb. They would treat us to visits to their summer home on Chocolate Lake, including boat rides on the lake. Another highlight was the small grocery store next door. Sometimes I was sent to buy an item or two for Mom. On one occasion this five year old decided to steal a nickel off the counter. When Mom found out, she strongly reprimanded me for the sin of stealing; I was promptly sent back to return the coin and apologize. I will never forget that lesson! I thank God that Mom dealt with me according to the Word of God and taught me to never take something that did not belong to me. The sting of correction reaped a godly fear of never stealing again.

The year 1946 saw us moving back to Hopewell Hill. I was six, and the beginning of my school days arrived. In September I started first grade at the Hopewell Hill School, the same elementary school my father attended as a child. It was a "little red schoolhouse" situated on the top of a hill. Grades one through six all met in the same room and was taught by one teacher, Mrs. McGorman. There were no school buses and most provided their own transportation through walking. During the cold, snowy winter months, I sometimes got a ride to school with my Aunt Verna. Not in a car or bus – she drove the local school van bringing the children from Woodworth Settlement in the back roads of Albert County to the main road. Her mode of transportation in winter was a covered wagon sleigh pulled along by her horse. When I relate this to my grandchildren, they think I lived during the *Little House on the Prairie* days.

Springtime in Hopewell Hill brought longer days and increased sunshine, causing the snow to slowly melt. Before long, tin buckets were brought out by the residents, the maple trees were tapped, and the buckets hung on the trees to catch the sap rising from the roots brought on by the warm sunshine. The sweet, clear sap was collected and boiled down into delicious maple syrup. The sugar camps boiled large vats and it was fun to drizzle the boiled syrup over the snow and produce maple candy.

Summers in Hopewell Hill in my young years were filled with happy memories. Mom delighted in giving me birthday parties with all the trimmings. A hammock swinging at the side of the tittle green house added to the summer fun. My cousins Emeline, Alex, and Wilbur Metcalf, Treva Tingley, Hughie Woodworth, and Kenny Stevens were my closest friends. Emeline was old enough to be my babysitter. A favorite game of the cousins was Hide and Seek. One day I hid in an upper room in Great Grandpa's old barn where Wilbur locked me in. I panicked, shouted in fear, and was ready to throw myself out the window and land on a manure pile when the young pranksters came to my rescue.

The older cousins took me to the local swimming hole at the creek off the Memel Road. We walked the narrow gravel road, past Great Aunt Bell Woodworth's home, squeezed under the barbed wire fence, and skipped through the meadow as we tried to miss stepping on the thistles and "cow pies". At last, we arrived at the creek with its rustic wooden covered bridge overhead. Years later as a teenager of fifteen I was baptized in water at this same spot. My eleven year old sister Betty was baptized the same day. I recollect it being a grave occasion, but obedience in following the Lord brought peace and joy to my heart.

My dad planted vegetable gardens in the summer, followed by days of Mom canning the fresh produce for the winter months. Three summer delicacies of the region are samphire and goose tongue greens handpicked on the salty marshes of Albert County. These greens served with butter and a little vinegar is still a New Brunswick delicacy. The third is "Hodge Podge", made from the early garden produce – baby carrots, peas in the pod, new potatoes, green beans, and yellow beans – served with fresh cream and butter. My mouth waters even as I think about this gourmet fare.

The Newcombs immigrated from England and then migrated to the Maritimes via New England several centuries ago. One notable descendant is Simon Newcomb, astronomer and mathematician, who is buried in Arlington National Cemetery. He is considered to be one of the most influential astronomers of his time.

Great Grandpa, George Whitfield Newcomb, named after the famous English preacher George Whitfield, was a devout

Methodist. One of his daughters, Great Aunt Ivah said of him, "His consistent life and kind disposition has always been an inspiration to me". He owned the local general store that housed the Hopewell Hill post office. Later on, Great Aunt Ivah ran the store when Great Grandpa was no longer able to work. The store seemed to sell anything anyone would need, from work boots and socks to bologna and cheese. When I opened the door the familiar smell of creosote wafted from the floorboards. Sometimes, but not often, we were indulged with treats from the many candy jars sitting on the counter.

My sister and I loved to spend time with my great Aunt Nellie and great Uncle Austin Woodworth and our cousin Alden on their farm back in Woodworth Settlement. In her youth, Aunt Nellie had been a schoolteacher; she had a knack of telling the most interesting stories. I can visualize the little farmhouse with its particular aromas—from cow dung, the chicken coup, and the pigsty. Each time I walked through the back porch to the kitchen the loose floorboards squealed and clanked. I wondered why Uncle Austin never repaired the floor.

Eggs to gather from the chicken coup, apples to pick in the orchard, butter to churn, and picking wild raspberries were some of my warm memories. I also recall pumping water in the kitchen sink where everyone drank from the same dipper. Red geraniums in shiny tin cans lined up like sentries on duty in the living room windows. Sometimes I was given the privilege of playing the antique pump organ in the corner of the living room. Aunt Nellie was my Sunday school teacher at the local Pentecostal church and she narrated Bible stories in a way that kept your undivided attention.

In the spring of 1947 my father, who was still serving in the Royal Canadian Air Force, announced to Mom, "I have been transferred to the remote town of Fort Saint John, in northern British Columbia".

I don't recall that Mom was disturbed at the prospect of such a major change in her life. I remember some of the preparations, such as storing our furniture in the local village hall also known as Solomon's Temple. The Air Force provided furniture for us. We proceeded to make that long journey to our new home situated about fifty miles north of Dawson Creek on the Alaska Highway. We never would return to live in the *Little Green House That Grew*.

It was a five-day train journey from Moncton, New Brunswick to Edmonton, Alberta, including a transfer to another train in Montreal. Our own compartment gave us privacy as the train's wheels clacked across the great Canadian expanse. Excitement filled the hearts of two little girls as we gazed at the passing panorama.

We were happy travelers whizzing by lakes, through seemingly endless forests, prairies, villages, towns, and cities. Is Canada really this big? Edmonton, Alberta finally came into view. From there, we took our first airplane journey to our final destination in the northern Canadian bush country. No sooner had we taken off from Edmonton when the plane suddenly returned to the airport with engine trouble. We stayed at a guest house over night. As children, we seemed to roll with the punches and the delay was taken in good spirits by our mother. We arrived the following day without further incident, greeted by Jimmy, an enormous, friendly crow. We were ready to begin life in the Canadian northwest, sparsely populated in the 1940's. Our new home was a military barrack converted into family living accommodations. Mom always seemed to adapt well to any and all changes that came her way. Our young lives were full of adventure.

Fort Saint John in the 1940's was a pioneer town with elevated wooden sidewalks and dirt roads like you see in western movies. The few shops on the main street included the Condell Hotel, a butcher shop, grocery store, cinema, and one restaurant. I recall a small cottage open to visitors to rest and use the restroom; it was run by a dear Christian lady, Mrs. Bessborough. The Air Force base, located four miles from town, meant transportation to and from school either in a bus or via an Air Force military vehicle. Winters were extremely cold with snow piled high, reaching the top of the telephone poles after the snowplows had cleared the way. I got my first pair of ice skates and learned to skate at the local air force rink despite suffering frostbite on my toes from time to time.

My mother soon found the only Pentecostal church in our new town. She quickly got involved, played the piano, taught

Sunday school and helped in whatever way she could. It was a small mission church pastored by Elmer and Ruby Clark. The young woman who assisted them not only had a colorful name, Miss Cowper-Smith, but an adventurous personality that kept our undivided attention with her story telling. One story that is indelibly printed on my mind was her desire to have a thousand children by opening an orphanage one day. Her future did bring forth a husband and many children through orphanage care.

Pastor Clark's ministry had a life-changing impact on me. One memorable, bitterly cold Sunday night, December 26th, 1948, as I sat in the service with Mom along with only a few attendees on that extremely cold night, the Holy Spirit dealt with my heart. I knew I needed to receive Jesus into my life and be born again. No sooner had I sensed my need of a Savior than Pastor Clark asked me, "Barbara, do you want to ask Jesus into your heart tonight and be born again?" Through tears I quickly said, "Yes", and knelt by my chair and prayed with the pastor. At once I knew I was cleansed, free from sin, and right with God. What a peace flooded the heart of this eight year old!

Mom was the one who taught us the Word of God at home. She read us Bible stories from the *Hurlbuts Story of the Bible*. The photos helped us to retain what she read. Mom also taught us to memorize Scripture and prayed with us each night. My background in the Pentecostal churches gave me a fear of the

Lord and a respect for Who He is. I am grateful for that aspect of my faith heritage. Some of the fear was not as godly as I once thought; it was a fear of man and consequences if I broke any of the many religious rules. Over the years I have learned the difference. The religious rules and spirit of condemnation contributed to my serious nature when I was a child. There were fun times, but most of the time I wondered if what I was doing was wrong. Sin consciousness is a terrible bondage.

My sister and I benefited greatly from Mom's domestic teaching skills. Her instructions made life so much easier when we became wives and mothers. We cooked and baked with her from the time we were little girls; cleaning up was part of our lessons. Sewing, knitting, and embroidery were fun activities too.

Dad bought his first car in 1947, a brand new shiny, navy, four door Chevrolet sedan. We thought we had arrived. Sunday afternoon drives during the short summer season with long sunny days were delightful. My sister and I longed to take a picnic lunch and stop by a stream to play and enjoy the scenery. But could we take a picnic? Of course not; it was Sunday and you didn't have picnics on a Sunday! I could never figure it out—what kind of sin would that be? This is an example of the type of religious rules I grew up with. No toys or dolls were allowed to be brought out on Sundays, only our coloring books. Sundays were not my favorite day of the week. Mom told us how when she and Dad were first married the church said it was wrong to have a Christmas tree. They ignored the admonition and brought a little tree into their home and decorated it with strung popcorn. We always enjoyed our Christmas trees.

Movies? They were definitely prohibited. In grade three our class was taken to see *The Wizard of Oz* at the Fort Saint John cinema. I happened to be sick that day and heard about it when I returned to school. My logical conclusion was that God allowed me to be sick, thereby preventing me from partaking in the sin of going to a movie. This sounds senseless today but that was serious Pentecostal doctrine. We were taught if the rapture took place and you were in a movie theatre you would be left behind!

The summer of 1948 included a long road trip back to the Maritimes where we enjoyed a Newcomb family reunion in Hopewell Hill and a visit back to Mom's roots in Sable River, Nova Scotia. We spent many days on the road, stopping in Kindersley, Saskatchewan to visit our great Aunt Mary and great Uncle Ernie Atkinson. Driving through the United States from this point on meant better roads. Our oasis of rest was in Royal Oak, a suburb of Detroit, Michigan where we stayed with Aunt Verna and Uncle Stillman Stone and daughter Jaunita. Their large home comfortably housed us, plus they had a television, the first one we ever viewed. Eating out and shopping was such a fun treat. City life was good!

One of the many blessings of Pentecostal teaching is that I learned about divine healing at an early age. Our mother prayed for us when we were sick. One particular incident stands out in my mind when we lived in Hopewell Hill. I had contracted whooping cough. Mom and the church members prayed for me and I was supernaturally healed by the power of God. All the symptoms left within a day.

There were many gaps in the teaching on the subject of healing, such as, not understanding the believers' authority in preventing sickness through faith and the confession of the Word of God. Another misconception was the belief that perhaps God sent the sickness to teach you something, therefore you couldn't be sure if you should pray against the sickness or not.

The baptism in the Holy Spirit with the evidence of speaking in other tongues was taught to me from an early age. Here again, lack of Biblical teaching on how to receive this wonderful gift kept me from receiving until six years after I was saved. According to the instructions I received I would cry, beg, and plead with Jesus at the church altars, along with others, and then walk away, each time disappointed. I did not understand how to simply believe, receive, and speak out in faith.

One Pentecostal church told me I wasn't "fully saved" unless I had received the baptism in the Holy Spirit and because I wasn't yet fully saved I would not go to heaven in the rapture if Jesus came. That erroneous teaching struck terror in my heart; I feared the rapture taking place and I would be left behind. I struggled with this and the teaching that I was unworthy. I cannot recall the righteousness of the believer being taught. This resulted in an unhealthy sin consciousness and a sense of unworthiness. This was extremely hard for a preteen child to spiritually process.

In spite of the lack of good teaching on how to receive the baptism in the Holy Spirit, I finally dared to believe Jesus to do what He said He had promised to do–to cease begging and simply receive the promise of the Father. At the age of fourteen I received this wonderful gift just like in the book of Acts and spoke in other tongues for the first time on May 24, 1955 in a little Pentecostal church in Summerside, Prince Edward Island. My sister Betty at the age of ten received two evenings later and we were both now "tongue talking" Pentecostal girls. Betty experienced an added blessing–she prophesied as well as speaking in tongues. She prophesied events concerning our father's restoration to the Lord which took place many years later.

I was not taught that the baptism in the Holy Spirit is the beginning of a life of walking in the Spirit; the gateway to a walk in the Spirit for the rest of my life. Since I was not instructed to pray in tongues in my private fellowship with the Lord, I missed out for a time on the value of being built up and edified in my spirit. The only time I thought I could or should speak in tongues was when I was at the church alter seeking God, or when I felt I should, rather than choosing to do it like Paul said he did, regardless of feelings. First Corinthians 14:15 states, "I will pray with the spirit, and I will pray with the understanding also: I will sing with the spirit, and I will sing with the understanding also."

The first time I heard teaching on the importance of praying in tongues on a daily basis was through Oral Roberts television ministry. It took time for this to become a personal revelation to my heart.

The year 1949 to 1950 brought us once again to Halifax, Nova Scotia. Dad was transferred from Fort St. John, British Columbia to the beautiful province of Prince Edward Island, nestled in the Northumberland Strait between Nova Scotia and New Brunswick. As our house was not ready on the Summerside Air Force base, we lived with my maternal Grandparents, Edgar and Cecelia Giffin, where my brother Audley was born. It was a happy year. The hours and days spent with Grandma Giffin were special. She took time to help me with homework and to develop my reading skills.

When we passed the Northwest Arm, an inlet off Halifax Harbor, we were quite impressed when Mom told us she swam across it as a young woman. A half kilometer is an impressive distance from a child's outlook.

I now lived closer to my Giffin cousins. During that summer I spent a special time with Rosemary, Judy and Johnny Giffin, with memories of staying at their large farmhouse in East Chezetcook, home of Uncle Russell and Aunt Bessie Giffin. It was my first experience to dig clams when the tides were low on the Eastern Shore of Nova Scotia.

Grandma Giffin related stories to me of her time spent in the United States as a young woman. She told how she worked as a "lady in waiting" in The White House for Louise Taft, the mother of President William Howard Taft. How important that sounded to a nine year old. Grandma was a "home body", meaning she hardly ventured outside the home in her later years. In contrast, Grandpa Giffin loved his Pentecostal Holiness church and proudly greeted the people at the door of the church whenever there was a service.

Grandpa was a tall, dignified man whom people said looked like King Edward VII, with his distinguished goatee. He worked fifty years as general manager and accountant for Moirs, a large Canadian bakery and confectionary company. Grandma had to line his pockets with cellophane as they were always filled with candy and goodies. Grandpa was a man of few words, so we never had much conversation with him growing up. We heard stories of how he had come out of the Baptist Church when he received the baptism in the Holy Spirit. One miracle related to me was how the Lord supernaturally protected him during the Halifax Explosion of 1917.

The *SS Mont Blanc*, a French cargo ship, carrying explosives bound for Bordeaux, France, collided with the *SS Imo*, a

Norwegian ship, in the Halifax harbor. This ship was carrying relief supplies to the war-torn nation of Belgium. The result was a great explosion with over 1,900 causalities and 9,000 injuries. At the time of this tragic accident, Grandpa was sitting at his office desk next to a large window in downtown Halifax. All the windows around him were blown out—except his! God protected him from this grievous blast that shook the nation of Canada. Mom says she vaguely remembers as a child of five the terrible impact it had on their home; the kitchen stove "danced" as if in an earthquake.

During fourth grade I attended the Le Marchant Street School in Halifax, the same school Mom attended. My sister and I spent many happy hours playing in the famous Public Gardens across the street from the stately apartment building where we lived with our grandparents.

"Always pray that the Lord brings the right person into your life. Just because he is a Christian man doesn't mean he is the one God has chosen for you." My mother's wise words often resounded in my ears. Mom taught me the importance of doing the will of God and it always stayed with me, especially in the matter of following His call on my life and a marriage partner. There was sensitivity in my spirit to the voice of the Lord, and I thank Him for His grace on my life from a child.

I remember the Lord speaking to me at the age of twelve in quite a profound way. As my father was driving us home from church one Sunday morning in Calgary, Alberta, I distinctly heard in my spirit words to this effect, "I am calling you to be a missionary." The nation of India loomed large in my mind. My response was normal for a twelve year old with dreams of a future with a husband and children.

I said, "But Lord, I want to get married and have children!" Going to India as a single missionary didn't quite fit in with my concept of serving God. I thought I would have to wear my hair in a "Pentecostal bun", dress in frumpy second-hand clothes, wear brogue shoes, and never be able to wear make-up or jewelry! Pentecostal missionaries and ministers certainly didn't present a great image for teenagers during that era. Missionary and marriage didn't quite fit together in my naive mind!

Over and over again I heard Mom say how she prayed that each of her children would serve the Lord. We had a constant prayer cover and it made a lasting impression on my life. I really did want to serve God and be in His will and follow His purpose for my life.

I believe Mom was often speaking out of her own experience. She felt she had missed the perfect will of God for her life by marrying my father (only the Lord knows if that was so). Her plans to attend Zion Bible School in Providence, Rhode Island, were interrupted by meeting my Dad. He had told her he would never interfere or stop her ministering. He had a vision of an open Bible and felt he also was called to preach. Unfortunately, he never matured spiritually as his mind was not renewed through a lack of good Bible teaching. He never dealt with the pain from his childhood as a result of his parent's divorce, and this was carried into their marriage. His disobedience to the call of God and wrong choices took him down the road of a life lived far from the blessings of the Lord. Our home life was not always the most peaceful place, and the atmosphere was often clouded with strife. Happy times were few and far between, and my mother lived under a lot of stress. I determined that I was not going to live that way or experience that kind of marriage. Obedience to the Lord was uppermost in my thoughts and in my spirit. My decision brought great rewards.

Chapter 4

Happy and Sad Times

During my childhood we moved so many times because of my Father's military work that it often seemed like a yearly event. Each New Year's when the Christmas tree was taken down, Mom would say, "I wonder where we will spend next Christmas?" And usually we were in another home on another air force base. The moves necessitated driving many miles across the country from east to west and vice versa. In the 1940's and 50's, the roads in the United States were much better than those in Canada. It was exciting to drive through the vast span of the western plains states, looking for the grain elevators on the horizon. The prairies, Mid-west, and beautiful sights of New England enriched my knowledge of the USA. I enjoyed reading the maps and took a great interest in each geographical area. I was excited to be on my way to our new home.

As I reflect on this, I realize how difficult it must have been for Mom. Again we stopped early enough in the evening to buy food for her to fix our evening meal in the motel and prepare breakfast the next morning. She also prepared sandwiches for our lunch on the road the next day. Rarely did we stop to eat at a restaurant; our Dad believed in the most economical way. Money was probably budgeted for the long journey. To eat out was a special treat.

I now appreciate how the frequent moves in my childhood prepared me for the future. Those experiences helped me to adjust and adapt to new places, friends, and situations. Somehow it never seemed a hardship but a great adventure. Since I changed schools so frequently, it probably had its downside with gaps in my studies, but I was unaware of any possible negative impact. My siblings and I were always ready to make new friends.

We lived in Prince Edward Island for two years and then headed west once again, this time to Alberta, staying the first six months in Calgary. I remember Mom taking me to an A.C. Valdez Healing Crusade where God's healing and miracle anointing was flowing. It made such an impact on my young life as I witnessed a goiter disappear and crossed eyes straighten. It was in Calgary in 1952 where the Lord spoke to my heart about becoming a missionary. Nine years later Calgary was to become a place where God gave me directions that totally changed the course of my life and destiny.

Dad was stationed in Claresholm, about one hundred miles south of Calgary. Our family lived in Calgary until our military home was ready on the nearby base in Ft. McLeod. A highlight of my time in Ft. McLeod was the birth of my youngest brother Elden, in June 1952. At the age of twelve, Mom felt I was responsible enough to help care for my baby brother, and it was such fun to play 'mother'.

In sixth grade in Ft. McLeod I met Barbara Demeter (nee Gibson), and we became best friends. She reminded me many years later how I shared with her my Christian testimony and told her how I felt God called me to become a missionary one day. Little did I realize at the time, my testimony was having an influence on her life. The seeds I sowed were to be watered by others; the Holy Spirit brought forth a harvest in her life years later. Barbara and I would dream of the things we would do when we grew up. She had a vivid imagination and this fueled late night conversations at our sleepovers. We often talked about writing books one day. She was a great inspiration. At the age of seventeen she and her boyfriend Les eloped. In years to come she and her husband were born again, baptized in the Holy Spirit, and opened a Christian bookstore. And I eventually wrote books! Barbara and I connected years later in 1986 when she heard my brother Elden give his testimony on *100 Huntley Street*, a Christian TV program in Canada. Elden mentioned I prayed with him over the phone from California when he recommitted his life to the Lord in 1982. It was through Elden's testimony that Barbara and I reconnected.

I recall the winter in Ft. McLeod as extremely cold with snow piled high over the doors and windows. Spring was especially welcomed that year. As the season changed this, too, meant change for our family. In May 1953 we were on the move once again, headed back to Summerside, Prince Edward Island.

Not So Merry Times

Our second two year stay in Prince Edward Island brought me to my teenage years. My Giffin grandparents from Halifax came to live with us in a three bedroom house with four children. It was a very difficult and stressful time for the family. In May of 1955, just after my sister and I were baptized in the Holy Spirit, we were presented with devastating news. The baptism in the Holy Spirit prepared us with supernatural strength for the traumatic events that were to follow.

Mom was faithful in serving in the local Pentecostal church; she was their pianist and ministered in song on their radio programs. Just after receiving the baptism in the Holy Spirit I was asked by the pastor to speak to the Friday night youth meeting. With my Mom's help, I came up with a message that lasted five minutes. I read it over and over as I watched the clock to see if I could possibly make it last a little longer. I had no idea this was the tiny beginning of my teaching ministry.

Dad often traveled to other air force bases in Canada in his engineering work as a troubleshooter for problems in the central heating plants on other bases. He arrived home after one of his trips to Newfoundland and announced to Mom that he was not only leaving her and the family but was divorcing her. It was such a shock to us all. Mom had four children to raise and support. Where would we go to live? What would we do? Where would Grandma and Grandpa Giffin go? I had just turned fifteen. Betty was soon to celebrate her eleventh birthday, Audley was five, and Elden only three years old. To make matters even worse, Dad announced that he was going to marry Mom's cousin. As I write of these events it sounds like something from a soap opera.

We finished our school year, but the events were so unpleasant all around. We believed the Lord would look after us, and in His faithfulness He prepared a place for us to live. My Aunt Gertrude (Dad's sister) and her husband Uncle Russell from Moncton, New Brunswick, suggested to Dad that he stay in their summer cottage in New Brunswick to give himself time to seriously think about what he was doing. Dad's response was that Mom and the children could go there to live instead. It seemed an easy way out for him to provide a home for us, but Mom took it to be God's provision for our family. My aunt and uncle agreed for us to go there, and the small summer cottage became our new home for nearly three years.

In July we waved goodbye to our Dad as we were leaving our home on the Summerside air force base. It was the saddest day of my life. We had no idea when we would see our Dad again. We were driven to Borden by one of Dad's employees to walk on the *Abeqweit Ferry* and cross the Northumberland Straight, a forty-five minute journey to Cape Tormentine, New Brunswick, where Uncle Russell met our beleaguered family.

We had happily traveled many times on this ferry but never without our father and in our own car. This was a humiliating experience. We felt rejected and abandoned by our father. The name *Abeqweit* is the Mi'Kmaq nations name for Prince Edward Island, meaning "cradled on the waves". Our family was soon to experience what it meant to be "cradled" in the loving care of our Heavenly Father.

We settled into our new home, a small, two-bedroom summer cottage in Riverside, only a short distance from the hospital where Betty and I were born. We had an indoor toilet but no bathtub or shower. The cottage had not been built to be used during the extremely cold Maritime winters. Mom made the best of our situation and thanked the Lord for a place to live. At least we had a kitchen oil stove and an oil heater in the living room to keep us warm in the winter. One winter the oil heater blew up resulting in oily black soot snowing on everything in our house.

Our aunt and uncle were incredibly good to us. My understanding is they did not charge rent as they knew even though

Dad sent financial support each month, it was never enough to meet the needs of five people. Mom kept her faith strong, and we learned to believe God for all our needs and a few wants. My industrious Mom did her part and planted a garden one summer. She canned and preserved everything she could get her hands on, and that helped us during the long winter months. Her sewing skills assisted as well to bring in a little income. We were poor but didn't know how poor we were as others around us didn't seem to have too much more than we did. Not many affluent people lived in the neighborhood. It was the 1950's and country life was slow and simple.

September arrived, and it was time to start school at the Riverside Consolidated School. I was in tenth grade. A few of my classmates were cousins, and I soon made new friendships, too. Most of my girlfriends were Baptists, and I was one of the few Pentecostals. There was the stigma of coming from a broken home. Divorce was almost unheard of during that era, especially in a small country community. People knew my Dad well as he had grown up there.

Divorce? Well, my Dad didn't actually get a legal divorce in Canada. He decided to go to the Reno, Nevada, marry our Mom's cousin, and then came back to live in Canada as a bigamist! The shame of this took its toll on us.

I share this to show you how later on in my Dad's life, the Lord had such mercy on him. Through all the events and suffering which came to our family as a result of my Dad's wrong choices, I continued to love him, pray for him, and forgive him. God's grace enabled me to deal with bitterness and unforgiveness. I learned to honor my Dad as the Scripture admonishes, but his sinful lifestyle grieved me.

Did the divorce affect me? Of course it did. I had to deal with rejection and insecurities as I grew up. Divorce always takes its toll on the children. But somehow God put a hedge around me and preserved me in so many wonderful ways. With the power of the Holy Spirit and a growing knowledge of the Word of God, I was able to deal with these issues as I matured in the Lord.

We carried on with our life in the Maritimes, which unfortunately became the sad times for us as a family. I continued with my high school education and began to dream of the future, but it looked so hopeless in our limited financial circumstances. I thought of attending college in Fredericton, New Brunswick, to become a schoolteacher. Then my heart would lean toward God's calling on my life, and I wondered how I could ever attend Bible School. I really didn't see my future amounting to much. I did think maybe I will marry a local guy and end up having many children.

We attended the local Pentecostal Church, the same one my Mom helped pioneer years earlier. It was painfully legalistic. I thought nearly everything I did was sin. I call it "negative religious works." We wanted to do what was right, but our minds were filled with "Don't do this and don't do that."

Happy and Sad Times

One Sunday I went to the lake with a family from the church, and enjoyed limited recreation, but not for long. When my mother and the church folks heard about it, I was strongly reprimanded. My Baptist girlfriends seemed to be much happier. Listening to pop music on the radio was not allowed, much less attending a movie. I listened to country music and Pat Boone when I could, and that was even looked down upon.

We didn't have a television, and it had only been made available in Canada in the 1950's. It meant we went to a neighbor's house to watch *I Love Lucy* or the *Perry Como Show*. One winter Sunday afternoon my sister took off to the neighbors to watch the next episode of "Lucy." Betty stood too close to the wood burning potbelly stove and burnt her only winter coat! She was scared to tell Mom as she was not only watching TV, but doing it – of all times – on a Sunday!

We had fun chopping down our Christmas trees in a nearby snowy field, resembling a scene from Currier and Ives. One year, Christmas happened to fall on a Sunday, and Mom decided to retain her religious tradition. We were not allowed to open our gifts that day. We had to wait until Monday! It all sounds silly, but at the time Mom was quite serious and tried to justify it in her way. We now can chuckle at this experience.

One Christmas stands out in my memory. There wasn't extra money for Mom to buy gifts. So what did she do? When the Sears Christmas Wish catalog arrived with all the exciting things children long for at that time of year, she simply prayed with us and taught us to believe the Lord would provide. Our young brothers wanted bright yellow Tonka trucks. There was no way Mom could buy them, even at $3.99 each. A big basket arrived at our house just a few days before Christmas. What surprises were awaiting us! On Christmas morning, we happily opened our gift, and much to the joy of Audley and Elden, their gifts were the exact trucks they had prayed for! God had spoken to a long time friend of Mom's to send us Christmas gifts – she knew nothing of my brothers' desires. Many notes of praise and joy ascended to our Heavenly Father. We experienced His Loving care over and over again.

Although money was painfully tight, Mom had a creative side. She brought a little pizzazz into our lives one Christmas. She indulged my sister and I in helping her make homemade chocolates – such a luxury indeed! I am sure the food budget suffered that month. We never knew. It was a temporary relief from the poverty surrounding us.

During the summer school holidays of 1957, I worked in the home of a lawyer and his wife in Moncton. This helped me buy back to school clothes. At the end of August, I had the happy privilege of being a bridesmaid for my cousin Beatrice Trimper (nee Pierce) in Digby, Nova Scotia. Again, no money to buy a dress, but God provided. I borrowed one.

My senior year in high school began in September 1957. During the time we lived in Riverside, I only recall my Dad visiting us twice in three years. One day in early 1958 our wonderful neighbor, Margaret Lutes, came to tell Mom she had a long distance phone call, as we didn't have a phone. When Mom returned she announced that Dad was on his way from Toronto, Ontario to visit us. He had left the air force and was working at a large Toronto hotel as a stationary engineer where he had met a Christian man who witnessed to him and invited him to Stone Church.

He said to my mom, "I have come back to the Lord, and I want to get back together with you and the children." It came as a complete surprise even though we had prayed for Dad's return to the Lord and ultimate restoration of our family unit. Dad arrived a few days later, and our whole world was turned upside down once again. Emotions ran high, and I remember my sister and I being extremely disturbed. We cried ourselves to sleep at night as we wondered what was going to happen to us. Some of the questions that kept going through our minds were, "Was Dad for real? Did he really come back to the Lord? Did he really break off his ungodly relationship? What was going to happen to the family now?"

Dad persuaded Mom to go to Toronto for a visit where they would arrange a future for us. He bought a house and they proceeded to start all over again. Events took place so quickly that within a month we were on a flight from Moncton to Toronto in a terrible snowstorm. It was February 14, 1958. We had a new home, new life, and new future. It was also a storm of emotions.

After our years in the Maritimes, life in the metropolitan city of Toronto was culturally different, and it took time to adjust. We felt awkward and insecure in our new surroundings. Our new home was located in the suburb of Agincourt. My sister and brothers resumed their schooling, but my dad asked me to work to help the family financially. He helped me get a job in downtown Toronto at the Bell Telephone Company. I quite enjoyed working and learning office and administrative skills. Later on, I attended night classes at a business college that proved to be a real asset in the secretarial world.

I believe the move to Toronto was of the Lord as there were many opportunities for us living in the city. If we had stayed in New Brunswick, I really don't know what my future would have held. In Toronto, our family became involved in the Stone Church. I made good friends among the young people. Sadly, my Dad discontinued going to church. He lapsed into his old ways and seemed unable to maintain a relationship with the Lord. This had a negative impact on my parents' marriage. Mom didn't know how to handle the situation, but she continued to go to church. Unfortunately, there was no Christian marriage counseling available at that time.

Later a Pentecostal church was planted in Agincourt where Mom became involved in playing the piano. Stone Church was a real blessing to me, and I continued to grow spiritually under the ministry of Pastor Fred Parlee. I gained confidence and learned to overcome my shyness in the young peoples'

Sunday School class. Initially, when I was asked to read the Scripture lesson, I was nervous and timid. I joined the choir and began to enjoy life and fun times with Christian young people who were not legalistic.

A visiting missionary at Stone Church made such an impression on my life. I cannot recall his name, but I do remember his message, challenging young people to totally dedicate their lives to serve the Lord. I responded to his invitation and went forward with many other young people that Sunday morning. I made a commitment to serve the Lord and do His will.

Among my lasting friendships at Stone Church are Lillian Di Marco and Ruth Nicholson (nee Grantham). Ruth arrived from Australia in 1959, and we soon connected. She invited me to see the movie *Ben Hur*. I was nineteen years old and had never been to a movie. Remember my Pentecostal legalistic teaching? With trepidation I joined her and kept praying the rapture wouldn't take place until the movie was over. Well, the Lord didn't come and I got more liberated from legalism.

In the spring of 1960, Ruth and I found ourselves making plans to move west to Calgary, Alberta. I don't quite recall how it all came about but we felt change was at hand, and we were ready to make the move if it was the Lord's will. Ruth's friend, Jane Price, from Pittsburgh, Pennsylvania, wanted to join us. Jane's job was coming to a close, and she felt she should come. In May of that spring, the three of us left by train from Toronto's Union Station and headed west. God was indeed leading us, and we were all going to experience surprising blessings from the Lord.

Ruth, a nurse, soon found work in a Calgary hospital. Jane worked for a Christian chiropractor, and I was employed in the personnel department at Calgary's City Hall. We shared a lovely apartment and proceeded to find a good Pentecostal church. Remember how the Lord had spoken to me at the age of twelve in Calgary? Well, we started attending the same full gospel church where my family attended years before. The same pastors, Rev. and Mrs. Frank Kosick, welcomed us. They were so good to us, treating us like their own family. We often joined them for Sunday dinner.

It wasn't long before Ruth was dating one of the young men in the church, and by the time November rolled around she and Tom Nicholson were married. Jane and I were excited to be her bridesmaids. Shortly afterwards Jane went off to Australia and married Ruth's brother David; they had been dating in Pittsburgh. He had returned to Sydney a short time before our move to Calgary. So many plans were fitting into place.

At the beginning of 1961, I was wondering what God had in store for me. First of all, I felt led to apply for Jane's job at the chiropractor's office and in faith bought my uniform before I was hired – that was a God incidence. I contemplated attending a Bible school in Saskatchewan, but I soon knew this was not in God's plan.

One day early in 1961, while working at the chiropractor's office a friendly Christian woman, Lillian Swanson, came in and began conversing with me. Lillian told me how she lived in London, England and was involved in promoting Sunday School materials in the churches of the United Kingdom and Europe. For no reason, other than God, she invited me to stay with her if I ever came to London. My heart felt an excitement and witness that this just might be the opportunity that God had for me. I thanked her for her kind invitation and took her address in case I should proceed in this direction.

Within weeks, I wrote Lillian to say I was coming to London. I had a strong desire to move there and a witness in my spirit that this was the direction I should take. Preparations quickly followed – I found the nearest travel agent and booked a one way ticket to England on the passenger ship, the *Empress of Canada*. In 1961, it was the most economical way to travel. It was a step of faith, and in May I was ready to embark on the journey that changed the direction of my life. Imagine my excitement at the prospect of travelling to England on the second voyage of this newly launched liner.

The month of May soon came with signs of spring and a new beginning. I made preparations to go home to be with my family in Toronto for three weeks. For this part of the journey, I traveled by bus, the least expensive way to travel. For three days I journeyed through all kinds of stormy, cold weather across the prairie provinces, south through St. Paul,

Minnesota, on to Chicago and Detroit before I arrived at my family home in Scarborough. My Mom seemed to have a peace about my decision, but my sister Betty felt sad not knowing when she would see me again. My brothers were young, and I don't recall them expressing their feelings one way or the other. I felt a little sadness knowing I would miss my brothers' growing up years. My Dad didn't express much emotion or opinion.

On the day I departed from Toronto Dad took me to the bus station to meet my dear friend Lillian Di Marco, who accompanied me to Montreal where we spent the last night before I embarked on the journey to a new and unknown life in England. Through streams of ticker-tape and many tears, I waved goodbye to my dear friend from the deck of the ship.

Chapter 5

Adventurous Beginnings in England

Purchasing a one-way ticket on the *Empress of Canada* demonstrated how serious I was about my move to another country and culture. There was no doubt in my spirit or mind that I was moving in the direction of the Holy Spirit for my life. I didn't understand much of what was happening, but I knew I was being led of the Holy Spirit. In the natural realm, it didn't make sense to leave my family. However, a great peace in my heart gave me confidence to move forward.

My first glimpse of the old world was the morning I awoke to view the beautiful green, lush hills of Northern Ireland and then sailing onward to the spectacular panorama of bonnie Scotland. The sun was shining in full spring brilliance. What a welcoming sight. The *Empress of Canada* sailed up the Clyde River to disembark its passengers via a tender boat at Greenock. After six days on the Atlantic Ocean, the final stop would be the following morning in Liverpool, England.

I was emotionally excited, even though so many unknowns lay before me. After I went through immigration and gathered my few suitcases, I boarded the train for London's Euston Station. The train seemed dark and grungy, but I took in all I could as the sound of the steam engine and clickity-clack of the carriages on the rails bore me toward London. I absorbed the new sights of the beautiful, quaint English villages and verdant countryside. The houses seemed small and close together.

Within a few hours, I arrived in London and was ready to begin my new life. The first night was spent at the nearby Bonnington Hotel off Russell Square. In the morning, I looked for a restaurant for breakfast, ignorant of the fact that breakfast was included in the price of the hotel room. I was soon aware of the peculiar aromas of London, particularly the diesel exhaust from the hundreds of black London cabs. When winter came, "pea souper" fogs arrived in the city. This, another new experience, was from the coal heating fireplaces that spewed blackish air pollution from each chimney.

The following day Lillian Swanson met me at the hotel. Her little English car barely held my luggage, but she lovingly welcomed me to her flat in nearby Islington. It consisted of three rooms on the third floor of an old Victorian vicarage located on Barnsbury Square. The little nearby park was filled with large trees that gave the impression that I was not living in such an old, congested city. The vicar and his wife lived in Canada for a season, and a warm welcome was extended to their Canadian visitor. It was a transitional time until I found my own accommodation, a bed sitter, located near the impressive Hampstead Heath in North London. This was my first London home. I could view the west end of London from the Heath on a sunny day.

I found the first few days culturally overwhelming; London seemed so busy and teaming with people. It was time to look for a job. I boarded a double-decker bus to the west end of the city. Within a short time I started secretarial work for Union Carbide Company off Piccadilly, not far from the famous Berkley Square. I never did hear "the nightingales sing", as the famous song proclaimed. In my heart, I had a song and peace knowing that I was in the right place at the right time. I knew I had not made a mistake moving to London.

I later went on to work for the president of a tea-and-coffee import-and-export company on Mincing Lane, not far from Tower Bridge and the Tower of London in the old City of London. It gave me further experience in learning the ways of British culture and business. I soon felt comfortable travelling the underground—also known as the tube—to work. It was crowded with business women and dapper English businessmen donned in their pin-striped suits and bowler hats, toting black umbrellas, rain or shine.

I began to learn British colloquialisms, quite fascinating to my young mind. For instance, the term "kippers and curtains". The British people are traditionally quite private. So they put up nice curtains to hide what is behind the windows to make it look like they are affluent, all the while they are eating kippers, a lowly inexpensive salted fish!

My world-view was evolving, but more importantly, my Christian world-view was expanding its horizons. My brief time attending St. Andrews Evangelical Anglican Church in Islington opened my narrow vision to recognize God had many believers in other denominations. The vicar's outreach included open-air meetings on the streets of his parish, and I was privileged to be a part of that ministry. A visit to the China Inland Mission in London, founded by Hudson Taylor, brought a greater awareness of missions in the world. I knew I was being changed – little by little.

One day I had a phone call from a Christian woman who asked me if I would be interested in working for a Christian solicitor (lawyer). It sounded promising, and I applied for the position. The Lord opened the door and I was now working for Mr. Graham Brims Ross-Cornes at a law firm situated on The Strand opposite the prestigious Royal Courts of Justice. The bells of the Church of St. Clement Dane, an island fifteenth century church in The Strand, named because of its locale in the middle of the street. Bells daily ring out the familiar nursery melody, "Oranges and Lemons." I was now surrounded by the British legal world.

I was thousands of miles from my simple, down-to-earth beginnings in New Brunswick. The "old world" was now my "new world".

Chapter 6

Revelations and Romance

Gordon was not aware that I had also attended the meetings in Spurgeon's Tabernacle, the Morris Cerullo tent crusade at the Elephant Castle, and the Oral Roberts Crusade in South Wales. I had casually observed him and thought perhaps he was of Italian or Spanish background with his handsome dark, wavy hair. He certainly didn't look like your typical Englishman. I was surprised to learn he was Welsh. These meetings happened prior to my introduction to Gordon at the London Revival Crusade in August of 1963.

I learned firsthand about the nation of Wales from Mr. Jones, my ninth grade music and Latin teacher in Prince Edward Island. He told the class heartwarming stories of the country of his birth – the land of song, ancient castles, coal mines, lush green mountains, fishing villages and fish and chips. I dreamed that someday I might visit Wales and experience its ancient and fascinating history.

The first Sunday back to church in September after my holiday in Cornwall brought a sense of excitement to my heart. "Did Gordon receive the post card? What would be the next step?" When the afternoon service ended, my heart was filled with anticipation as Gordon approached me.

"Would you like to go for tea this evening"?

My heart pounded as I quickly replied, "Yes".

It was a beautiful sunny September evening as we strolled along Park Avenue toward Marble Arch to the corner of Oxford Street. It seemed so right to be together. We enjoyed tea time at the famous Lyons Tea House. Afterwards he accompanied me to my residence in north London. The entire evening was so special, and the Holy Spirit witnessed to our hearts that we were being drawn together in God's divine plan.

As the evening concluded Gordon went his way home to East Molesey, but not before gently kissing me – to me it was a token of his commitment and a seal of our lives together forever.

Our love began to blossom as we continued seeing each other after church on Fridays and Sundays. It didn't take long for Gordon to express his love for me and to discuss our future together. We spent time praying over each step – how and when to proceed.

I recall that when I first met Gordon, he was walking in a level of faith that challenged me. At the time he was an associate pastor and had gained much more knowledge and experience than I when it came to walking and living by faith in the Word of God.

When Gordon told me that we would be "living by faith" for the rest of our lives, I quickly agreed. It sounded quite spiritual as well as exciting. Little did I know then what I know today of the adventures of faith we would experience together as we served the Lord in many nations of the world.

I had limited knowledge and understanding when it came to living by faith, but I knew in my spirit it was the right way to live. As I wrote, it was through God's grace I took a few bold steps in believing God for direction in my life. One incidence was purchasing a one-way ticket on a ship from Canada to England. I knew in my heart it was God's will to move to London. And God certainly rewarded my faith. I was willing to do what God had called me to do and be where He wanted me to be without fully understanding the outcome. I had an increased hunger for a greater knowledge of the Word, so that I could please Him and live according to His Word.

At that time my understanding was that Gordon and I would trust God to meet all of our needs but not much more. The words "living by faith" presented a mental image that we would always struggle, barely getting by, not quite making it. We would have to be humble enough to receive the leftovers, wear hand-me-down clothes, drive old cars, and sit on second hand furniture. This belief was based on how I saw Pentecostal pastors live and barely survive in ministry. How little I knew at that time of the absolute goodness of God. We all begin where we are, but the Lord expects us to grow in grace, faith, and knowledge.

My thoughts were far from what God had in mind for us. I can see how my mind needed to be renewed, to think and talk like God (Romans 12:1,2). My concept at that time was not an accurate representation of a good and loving Heavenly Father. My beliefs were a reflection of my limited knowledge and understanding, combined with past religious teaching on the subject of living by faith.

I am happy to report that we have proved God's Word is true. In fifty years of marriage and full time ministry, He has taken pleasure in blessing us far beyond our greatest expectations and desires. Was this faith walk easy? No, it wasn't always trouble-free; we have faced many challenges and difficult times, but we were both committed to be faithful to the Word of God. He has rewarded us beyond what we asked or thought (Ephesians 3:20).

December 1963 arrived and we were three months into our relationship with a growing sense of God's hand upon our lives together. Gordon invited me to spend Christmas with him at his sister June's home in Cowfold, West Sussex. It turned out to be a blessed time, and we were able to minister to June. I continued to be used in the gift of tongues on a regular basis in church, and I asked the Lord to use me in the gift of interpretation of tongues according to 1 Corinthians 14:13.

The Lord granted my request. While visiting, the Lord had a word for June through the gifts of the Holy Spirit, comforting and edifying her, as well as showing her things He would do for her in the future. It all came to pass! What an encouragement this was to June and us as well.

Gordon and I talked about making our engagement official, but when? Two days after Christmas, we took the bus down to Brighton on the English Channel and walked around the various jewelry stores, looking at rings. Gordon purchased an engagement ring that day. God had supernaturally provided the money. It was not until the next day that he presented it to me on our way back to London. As we waited for our train on the platform of Horsham station on a bitterly cold, winter afternoon, he slipped it on my finger! My heart burned with joy and a great peace filled our spirits that we were proceeding in exactly the right direction.

More Revelations

In November of 1963, Selwyn Hughes announced that there would be an American speaker, Dr. Richard Carter, from Atlanta, Georgia, coming to the London Revival Crusade to minister. He was known as an anointed prophet of the Lord, who flowed beautifully in the revelation gifts of the Holy Spirit and in a strong prophetic anointing. We had never experienced a ministry like this. He ministered in the prophetic with the gifts of the word of wisdom and the word of knowledge. We were spell bound by the accuracy of the revelations. His authority in the Holy Spirit made us sit up and listen to what the Spirit was saying to the church.

During the Sunday afternoon service Dr. Carter suddenly stopped as he ministered to the line of people, turned around, looked at Gordon as he sat on the platform and said, "Young man, God has a word for you!" Gordon suddenly stood to his feet quite shaken by this unexpected word spoken with such authority. He proceeded to listen to the "word of the Lord". Never before had he experienced God speak into his life the way this anointed prophet ministered that day. From that moment on Gordon was a changed man; he was filled with a passion to fulfill the calling God had on his life. These are the anointed words that went into Gordon's spirit:

> May I pray for you now please? Brother, this is the Lord. You want Christ, you want the fullness of what God has for you. You have coveted gifts of the Spirit and many times His fruits. There has already been a foundation laid, and tonight you will begin to see what our God will manifest shortly; that your God will use you, and that you will always be small in your own sight, that you will be able to lift Him up and make Him a big God in the eyes of others. I

Revelations and Romance

anoint thee in the name of the Father, Son, and Holy Ghost for the ministry my child that thou hast desired ...and limit not thyself by small things for there is no limitation, saith the Lord, where there is an honest heart. Therefore, leave thy heart open and honest before thy God and walk in the way of the Lord. For the Spirit of the Lord God is upon thee that you might know the perfect will of God, that thou mayest not be overwhelmed. Yield thyself unto your God and be thou able to praise Him who hath loved thee, in other languages and in the power of the Spirit. But also in the gift of discerning of other spirits, in the power of the gift of the word of wisdom, in the power of the gift of the word of knowledge, in the power of the gift of faith, shalt thou manifest the power of Jesus Christ in holy compassion, grounded in the love of God shall the Lord use thee. In the days before thee thou shalt see it. Keep a broken and contrite heart before the people, smitten with a burden for the lost. It will be a work of God; it will be an individual need to individual hearts and will smite your soul. It will not be a general thing; it will be a personal thing, saith the Lord.

This personal prophetic word spoke of Gordon's future ministry and gifting of the Holy Spirit that would flow through him – the word of wisdom, word of knowledge, faith, and discerning of spirits. The Lord said through this powerful prophetic word, which always remained with him, "You will always make God big in the eyes of others."

Not only did Gordon receive direction for the ministry office God had called him to, but it was a confirmation that he would be serving Him in full time ministry. One day, his employment with the Inland Revenue would cease. Gordon didn't understand when this prophecy would fully come to pass, and sometimes he felt a little frustrated that its fulfillment seemed so slow. Later, he received insight on the timing of the prophetic, and the responsibility he had to pray for its fulfillment. There is a due season. In God's time, the prophetic word came to pass, line upon line, as he moved into the various seasons of his ministry.

Chapter 7

Marriage and Ministry

A new year began, and the winter months turned into the spring of 1964, Gordon faced the death of his father. On Saint David's Day (The Welsh patron saint), March 1, Gordon's father suddenly passed away leaving his mother devastated. They had been married for 45 years. Soon afterward, Gordon and his mother moved into a house in Kingston-upon-Thames, Surrey.

We continued to seek the Lord as to our wedding date. We began a faith adventure in every sense of the word – not only when to marry but all the questions that arose concerning where we would live and how to make the transition from working in the secular world to serving in full time ministry. Praying "in the spirit" was a regular part of our times together; and in doing this we were praying out the will of God so it could be manifested in the natural realm. *"Praying always with all prayer and supplication in the Spirit ...* (Ephesians 6:18).

By the time June 1964 arrived, we sensed it was time to set a date for our wedding. We became man and wife on Wednesday, August 19 at 2 p.m. in the Elim Church in Kingston-upon-Thames, Surrey. The Elim church was Gordon's home church for many years before joining the London Revival Crusade. In 1985 when renovations were taking place in downtown Kingston-upon-Thames, the little Elim Church was torn down revealing ancient Roman ruins beneath the church, little did we know!

The Lord began to show Himself faithful and strong on our behalf in meeting our needs every step of the way. Marion Hall, who introduced me to Gordon, said her sister would loan me her beautiful ivory brocaded wedding dress. I purchased an ivory veil and headpiece to match the dress. It was classy and beautiful.

Two ladies in the London Revival Crusade took it upon themselves to bake a wedding cake for us. The traditional British wedding cake is a dark fruit cake, covered with marzipan and white icing. When they presented it to us a short time before the wedding, we graciously thanked them for their kindness, but somehow it just didn't look right. We felt an uneasiness about it, so one day we boldly cut into it and much to our dismay—it was raw on the inside! Now we had to figure out how to tell the ladies we could not use this cake, as they would be attending our wedding. It was a dilemma, but we decided to tell the ladies what we discovered. They apologized, and no one was offended. We quickly went to one of the local bakeries and ordered another cake in time for the reception.

Another need we had was to prepare Gordon's mother's home for the wedding reception. It needed to be redecorated. We prayed and the Lord sent someone to assist. There was a World War II bomb shelter in the back garden that needed to be demolished. Again the Lord sent someone to take care of that. Gordon's sisters and sister-in-law helped prepare the reception meal. It was a disappointment that no one in my family was able to travel from Canada to be with us on our special day.

We had developed a special friendship with Peter and Pamela Douglas, who also attended the London Revival Crusade. Peter at that time was a London "bobby", but he was soon to leave the London police force to go into full time ministry. We asked Peter to be my dad for a day and he kindly consented to give me away on our wedding day. Peter and Pamela became precious long time friends.

At last August 19 arrived, an overcast Wednesday, but the sun shone through by the afternoon. Our wedding was simple, and we sensed a real peace and anointing as Selwyn Hughes performed the ceremony and pronounced us "man and wife". After our reception, we left by train to the south coast for five days to spend our honeymoon in Elmer Sands, a little village near Bognor Regis, West Sussex on the English Channel. Years later, we returned to Elmer Sands to find the little hotel where we honeymooned turned into a nursing home. We laughed and commented that we wouldn't be paying them a visit!

Just a few days before our wedding, Gordon left his secure employment at the Inland Revenue for full time ministry. Selwyn offered him a job to work with him in the London Revival Crusade. Gordon led the Friday night meetings in Dennison House, called "The Faith Pool", ministering the Word and leading the people in prayer. A small office was set up for him in the Oxford Street administrative office. Gordon assisted Selwyn in his evangelistic outreaches in Leicester Square and the Soho region of London. They preached on the streets, and then invited the young hippie drug addict generation into the basement of the Orange Street Congregational Church for tea and refreshments. Many were saved when given the opportunity to receive Jesus into their lives.

Orange Street Congregational Church, located between Leicester Square and Trafalgar Square, has a rich history of revival dating back to the 1600's when first pastored by French Hugenots, followed by English pastors, including Augustus Toplady, author of the famous hymn, "Rock of Ages". Sir Isaac Newton, whose house was connected to the church, often attended the services.

The Lord began to use Gordon in ministering the baptism in the Holy Spirit through the laying on of hands. People quickly began speaking in tongues (Acts 19:6). This became a regular part of Gordon's ministry to the believers.

I left my legal secretary job on The Strand to fully support our ministry. Gordon no longer had the car he received through exercising faith in the Word of God when he was single. He had been led to give it to a couple he knew. Our mode of transportation was a Lambretta scooter. Gordon took me grocery shopping on it and even up to London for one of our meetings. We looked quite hip riding around on a scooter back in the '60's!

It was time to believe God once again for better transportation. We prayed and released our faith together for a good car. In a matter of weeks we were driving an Austin Westminster, one of the larger British sedans of that time. God again proved His faithfulness to us in meeting our needs.

Our accommodation was a three room flat, the upstairs of Gordon's mother's home. We excitedly fixed it to our liking, applying fresh paint and wallpaper. Flats or apartments were extremely scarce to rent in the 1960's, so we took this to be God's provision for us for a season.

The Full Gospel Businessmen's Fellowship International sponsored an airlift outreach to London in November 1965. We attended these meetings held at the Hilton Hotel on Park Lane in London, meeting such people as Oral Roberts, Rev. A.C. Valdez Senior, Nicky Cruz, Pat Robertson, and other people of God. I reconnected with Harris Webb and Rev. George Whitehurst from Halifax, whom I knew as a child.

The time had come for us to begin our own ministry. We called it Living Waters Revival Ministry and began to hold meetings in London. After searching for a suitable venue, a hall was located in Drury Lane not far from the theatre district in the West End of London. It was a rather dreary place on Drury Lane, to say the least. We did some door-to-door work, inviting the neighbors to the meetings on Sunday afternoons. We were zealous to reach people for Jesus. Dr. Richard Carter was back in London, and he came to speak for us on one occasion. He became a dear friend who would stay with us on his visits to England. He continued to minister into our lives, and we valued his friendship, encouragement, and prophetic ministry.

It was now August 2, 1966 and we were proud parents of our first born, a son, Jason Robert, born in Kingston Hospital. He brought great joy to our family. During one of Rev. Morris Cerullo's yearly London Crusades, we asked him to pray the prayer of dedication over his life. The words spoken that day have come to pass as we have witnessed God's blessings on every aspect of Jason's life.

Tickets to Nowhere

In 1967, Gordon and I were still living outside London in the small flat. We had been married for three years, full of enthusiasm for our present and future life in the ministry. Life was challenging as we were learning to believe God for our needs, and sometimes a little more. We had experienced supernatural provisions, and we knew how to believe God in certain areas. We did not realize how much we needed to grow in understanding how to operate in faith for finances. On this occasion, we stepped out way beyond our boundaries.

I had not been back to visit my family in Canada for six years, and Gordon had not met his in-laws. We prayed and planned for this wonderful trip of a lifetime to visit my parents and siblings. We were excited to show off our first born and introduce him to his Canadian grandparents and the rest of the family. We both *thought* it was the right time to take this trip to Canada. Jason was ten months old and full of life and personality. So down to the travel agent we went to plan this exciting trip. We booked our airline tickets in "faith" and expectantly waited for the money to come in to pay for them.

In fact, we waited right up to the last day. Nothing happened. No money meant there were no tickets to pick up. The travel agent phoned us and Gordon awkwardly told her to cancel our tickets. *Why?* We questioned God and each other. *Did God let us down? What happened?* God did not let us down; He is a prayer answering Father when we pray according to His will. We soon figured out we were in presumption. We *thought* it was the right time to make this trip. How wrong we were. Timing with God is so important. Embarrassed and even mortified, you ask? Oh yes, of course!

We had to tell the travel agent we didn't have the money and then notify my family in Canada we weren't coming. They were disappointed, and I am not sure they fully understood. We eventually got over the disappointment, accompanied by a brief time of depression. We learned a great lesson – not to run ahead of the Lord and act as if He had told us to do something when, in fact, He hadn't. It was our idea. We had no business trying to believe God for thousands of pounds for this trip, when we were struggling to pay our bills and meet our daily needs.

The farthest we could travel on the day we *thought* we were flying off to Toronto, Canada, was a short trip to the beach in Littlehampton, West Sussex, just forty miles away. We did eventually go to Canada in 1968, when we moved there with two young sons. How good and wise is our Heavenly Father. We learned to be led of the Holy Spirit, and listen to His voice as He led us in His perfect plan and purpose.

Chapter 8

Crossing Over to The Other Side

The following year we had another blessing—the birth of our second son, Russell Matthew on June 8, 1968. My pregnancy was unlike my first. I had upper back pain during the third trimester. My blood pressure was much too high, and I was not aware that preeclampsia, a serious condition, had developed. My due date arrived, and I had not gone into labor. The visiting midwife called the ambulance and advised me to go straight to the hospital. The result was an emergency caesarean section. It was a seriously critical situation, and if the surgery had been delayed by even fifteen minutes, we could have lost our son, and my life was also in jeopardy.

We give the Lord thanks for preserving my life and the life of our baby boy. Russell Matthew was a large baby, nine pounds, five and a half ounces. Praise God, we both recovered from the trauma of preeclampsia. After a six week check up the doctor said Russell's heart had fully recovered from the stress of the surgery. We knew God's hand was upon Russell as God spared his life. We now had two precious little boys and my work increased.

After Russell's birth, we felt it was time to find our own place, an apartment or a house. Nothing opened up, and we further sought the Lord for His direction. It seemed good to us and the Lord that we should relocate to Canada. We made all the necessary preparations. Gordon was accepted by the Canadian immigration authorities. We put our furniture up for sale, and it was not difficult to sell. There had been severe flooding in the area during September of 1968, and many people needed to replace damaged furniture. We were led to give our car to Peter and Pamela Douglas, who were now in full time ministry. We packed a couple of tea chests with our most important possessions, filled our suitcases, and the four of us left England on November 12, on the *Empress of England* from Liverpool.

It was rather wrenching for Gordon to leave his widowed mother, not knowing when he would see her again. But the Lord arranged for her to live next door to Gordon's brother Glynn and his wife Joan. She would not be alone. Also, Gordon's two sisters lived nearby. As we left that bright November morning, little Russell looked at Gordon's Mother and smiled as if to say, *All is well Nan, we will be back to see you.*

It was a faith adventure, but we knew the timing of the Lord was right and that He would provide for every area of our lives and ministry. Gordon had boasted to me that he wouldn't need the sea-sickness tablets I had purchased for the trip. After all, Gordon was British – Britannia rules the waves – or so he thought. We experienced a gale, force nine, during that autumn crossing. It turned out Gordon was sea sick nearly every day, and I was well. I couldn't afford to be sea sick, seeing I had to look after a five month old and a two year old.

Gordon was well enough on the Sunday to hold a Pentecostal service in the theatre. A few people came, and he preached the Word with boldness. During the turbulent seven days, crossing the Atlantic, the Lord spoke to Gordon and gave him important instructions to prepare him for future ministry. God's Word stayed with him for a long time: "See, I have this day set thee over the nations and over the kingdoms, to root out, and to pull down, and to destroy, and to throw down, to build, and to plant" (Jeremiah 1:10).

The Lord showed Gordon what the ministry of the Word of God and the Holy Spirit desired to accomplish through the pastoral ministry that lay ahead. It would require pulling down and destroying traditions and doctrines of men in order to build and plant the work of the Kingdom.

Six days later, on November 18, we arrived in Quebec. Just before our arrival, we received a telegram while docked in Quebec City. My father had paid for our train tickets from Montreal to Toronto. We praised God for this wonderful blessing. We left England with limited finances, knowing our

Heavenly Father would meet our needs every step of the way. Being in God's will gave us peace and confidence each day.

Exhausted after going through customs and immigration on our day of arrival in Montreal on November 19, we made our way to the train station and boarded a fast train to Toronto. It seemed so cold and wintery, when in reality winter had not yet begun. We were met at Union Station in Toronto by my parents. It was the first time for Gordon to meet them and for my parents to see their first grandchildren. It had been seven and a half years since I had left Canada. It was such a joyous reunion as we embraced each other. I left Canada single, and here I was returning with a husband and two small children.

We proceeded to my mother's apartment in Scarborough to be welcomed by my teenage brothers, Audley and Elden. My mother graciously opened her home to us to stay with her as long as necessary. We had no idea what the next step would be, but we were confident of the Lord's leading and provisions.

Gordon ministered in several of the Toronto Pentecostal churches, including Pastor Maxwell Whyte's in Scarborough. An Estonian Presbyterian Church and a Methodist Church also welcomed Gordon to minister. After an appointment with the General Superintendent of the Pentecostal Assemblies of Canada, Gordon was accepted to pastor one of their churches. We waited to see where we would be sent. We were willing to go anywhere the Lord desired. Gordon brought with him letters of recommendation, one from Rev. John Carter, whose church we had attended for a short time in Wimbledon. He is the younger brother of the famous minister Howard Carter of the Assemblies of God in England, better known in America for the classic book, *Spiritual Gifts and Their Operation*.

Gordon met one of the leaders of the Full Gospel Businessmen's Fellowship in Toronto, a Mr. Kroener, who invited him to one of the Toronto meetings where a large Russian delegation of businessmen had been invited to attend. It was amazing to witness these precious Russian people hearing the Gospel.

Gordon did a little *tent making* at the local post office over the Christmas season to meet the needs of the family. As February arrived, surprising and exciting events quickly unfolded.

Chapter 9

Georgia–Soon on our Mind

The winter of 1968-1969 in Toronto seemed long and cold. We were not accustomed to the extreme temperatures or piles of snow left by the winter storms. Staying in an apartment with two small children was a little frustrating, but we determined to seek the Lord. We knew He would open the right door for us at the right time.

During the month of February 1969, Gordon received the most amazing phone call.

"Brother Gordon," the deep voice came through from the other end of the line. It was our dear brother and friend, Dr. Richard Carter, of Decatur, Georgia.

Somehow he heard we were in Toronto, perhaps through his son David, whom we saw just before we left England. The remarkable thing about this call was that he had my (Barbara's) mother's phone number. We had no idea he even knew her name, and we were quite stunned by his call.

He quickly got to the point. "Brother Gordon, would you be willing to pastor a church in Georgia? There is a Southern Baptist Church just outside of Atlanta and they have been without a pastor for six months."

"Are you willing to come to Georgia?"

"Why yes, I am willing, if that is the Lord's will," Gordon responded. "You know I have a Baptist background; I was brought up in the Welsh and English Baptist churches."

Dr. Carter quickly replied, "I'll recommend you to the pulpit committee that the church vote you in as the pastor of Stewart Baptist Church and get back to you right away. If they confirm the vote, I'll drive up to Toronto and bring you and Barbara and the children down to Georgia. If the church doesn't vote in favor of you being their pastor, there is another possibility. I know a church in Minnesota that needs a pastor."

We felt a certain excitement about moving south to a warmer climate, but of much more importance was being in God's perfect will – whether it be the extremely cold winter weather of Minnesota or the warm, southern climate and hospitality of Georgia. "Lord, where would you have us go?" was our prayer.

It was a matter of days when the phone rang again. Dr. Carter related the glad news: Georgia was calling us! We need not invest in more heavy winter clothing and snow boots. Miracles were taking place that we did not quite fully appreciate at that time. This church had never heard Gordon speak, and the pulpit committee had not asked Gordon what he believed. Yet the church members voted Gordon to be their pastor. In the Southern Baptist tradition it was unheard of to call a pastor in this manner, but the church felt led to call Gordon to be their pastor, based on Dr. Carter's recommendation. It was really the voice of the Lord that caused them to make such an astonishing and unusual decision. We knew in our spirit we were to go.

Within two weeks, Dr. Carter arrived in Scarborough ready to drive us to our next assignment. He announced that he had bought us the car we were travelling in to Georgia, a 1961 Pontiac Bonneville. It looked so large and luxurious after driving a smaller British car. It was around the beginning of March 1969; our hearts were filled with excitement and joy as Dr. Carter drove us as a family to the sunny south.

Within three days, including stops in New York State, Pennsylvania, and Virginia, we safely arrived at our destination, Stewart Baptist Church. The Stewart community is located twelve miles south of the town of Covington, a beautiful southern town graced with historic plantations and southern antebellum mansions. The streets are lined with magnolias and large oak trees. Today the town has the reputation of being the Hollywood of the South; the location is ideal for movies. In the 1970's, *The Dukes of Hazard* television series was filmed there.

The church parsonage, a little white ranch style home nestled among the tall pine trees, was a welcome sight. Surrounding this small Georgia community, we observed vestiges of cotton fields and a cotton gin; it spoke of abundant cotton harvests in days gone by.

This was our first house since getting married. Previously, we had lived in small apartments in England. The furnishings of our home were sparse in the beginning but much appreciated. Our few boxes of personal items brought from England arrived a short time later. It was sheer joy to settle into our little home and make preparations for the pastoral work that lay before us.

Our little boys grew up in a culture quite different from their land of birth. Jason, two and a half, had acquired a vocabulary filled with British words and phrases, accompanied by a strong accent. He was soon to forget his "proper" English pronunciation. It was lost to the southern drawl in no time. Russell followed suit. We were all soon to experience a new culture and the slower place of southern living.

The warmer weather accompanied by high humidity in the summer was a challenge the first year. The church did not have air-conditioning when we first arrived. Cooling off in the church services was the old fashioned southern way—fanning oneself with paper fans provided by the local funeral home. When the temperature rose to 100°F with 100 percent humidity, it was a shock to our bodies. Gordon still maintained his British tradition of wearing a suit and tie, much to his discomfort.

We recall how we gradually adapted to cultural and racial differences. We arrived in the South during the integration of the schools. At that time, tensions ran high among the people; even white Christians were vocal about not wanting their children to attend school with the African-American children. There were marches in the local town, and the stores were boycotted for a time by the African-Americans. We had to use great discretion and wisdom and chose to show God's love during this sensitive transition. Racial prejudice was deeply engrained. It takes time for God to change men's hearts and beliefs.

Soon after arriving in Georgia while driving one day in downtown Atlanta, Gordon was apprehended by a woman who jumped in his car at a traffic light and shouted, "Quickly, drive here; go over there!" Not knowing what to do, Gordon kept following her directions, thinking it was some kind of emergency. Finally being told to stop in front of a house, the woman got out and shouted to him, "Wait." He decided it was time to go and quickly sped away, never knowing what it was all about. It was probably deliverance for Gordon from some sort of danger.

The southerners are known for their hospitality. The church welcomed us to the community with their gentle and loving warmth. Gordon started visiting his parishioners during the week. It was not unusual for the older people to relax on the front porches, rocking in their rocking chairs, chewing on snuff. Gordon had to watch which way the wind blew when they spit into their spittoons!

Gordon was introduced to his first fishing experience at the local lakes, catching catfish. Oh, how British he was – he actually wore a tie to go fishing. It didn't take long to enjoy the delicacies of the local restaurants – plenty of catfish, hushpuppies, and coleslaw. Another first was being diligent to watch out for snakes, big poisonous ones. One day while Gordon walked down by the river, a huge water moccasin slithered across his shoes. The hairs on the back of his neck literally stood on end!

Each Sunday before the service began the deacons and men of the church would gather outside the main door and indulge in their cigarettes or cigars. This was a "no-no" in our Full Gospel background, but we chose to graciously overlook it and let the Holy Spirit deal with them.

One afternoon Gordon paid a visit to J.W. Gunnells, the Chairman of the board of deacons. They talked together for a while, and when Gordon told him he must leave J.W. said, "Preacher, don't go; stay a while." He prevailed upon Gordon to stay longer, so he sat down and started conversing again. Two or three more times, Gordon indicated he would be leaving, and J.W. repeated the same words, "Preacher, don't go; stay a while." Gordon again stood up and sat down several times. He thought, "How do I leave without offending him?" Finally he said, "J.W. I really must go home; Barbara will have supper ready," and then politely excused himself and went on his way.

Gordon and I were obviously ignorant of the local customs and colloquialisms. We had no idea that the words, "Don't go; stay a while" really meant "Goodbye." The whole church heard of Gordon's dilemma, and those who still remember laugh about it today. When people came to visit us, they would say as they were leaving, "Y'all come go home with me now." We soon learned this is their way of saying "Goodbye"; we were not to take it literally. We thought, "What a strange way to communicate."

We did our shopping in the city of Covington, twelve miles away. A weekly treat was a visit to Dairy Queen, one of the few fast foods in town when we first arrived. On one occasion Gordon took the boys for a hamburger and ice cream treat. He had taught them to pray over their food and so proceeded to give thanks to the Lord as he did at home. No sooner had Gordon said "amen," when Jason, now a four year old, loudly shouted his concern.

"Dad, why do you pray loud at home and pray quietly when we come here?" Out of the mouth of young children!

It was the custom during the Christmas season to show children's movies at the cinema on the town square in Covington. This allowed the parents time to shop. Gordon took Jason and Russell to the scheduled movie one Saturday afternoon. He lingered at the back of the cinema waiting for the movie to start. Much to his surprise it was not suitable for young children. Before he could rescue them, he saw two little guys stand up and walk toward the door. Our young sons had the sense to get out; they knew it was not something they should watch. Gordon quickly reported it to those responsible, and the movie was quickly changed.

Chapter 10

Pulling Up, Tearing Down, and Revival

How in the world did we end up here in this little southern community? This is the other side of the story.

There was a dear Spirit-filled lady in rural Georgia, who kept her faith strong as she prayed for a Spirit-filled minister to pastor the Southern Baptist church she attended. No one in the church believed that divine healing and the baptism in the Holy Spirit were for us today. Mrs. Mitchell persevered for twenty years, believing God would send a pastor to teach the full gospel truths. This dear lady never gave up as she prayed persistent faith-filled prayers over the years. God heard her prayers in the Spirit and set His plan in motion. It took twenty years. You see, God had to work on our end and position us to be in the right place at the right time, so we could fit into His plan. The phone call Gordon received that morning in Toronto changed not only our lives but the people to whom God sent us to minister to. Gordon soon realized he was the answer to the prayers of this dear lady.

Our mission began as we boldly taught the full gospel message to the people. For seven and a half years we ministered the Word with many signs following (Mark 16:17-18). The whole county was affected by the supernatural move of the Holy Spirit as revival fires spread to those who were spiritually hungry. This move of God was not without persecution, but the fruit that ensued was absolutely astounding.

In the beginning of Gordon's pastoral ministry at Stewart Baptist Church, it seemed the Lord did not reveal many details to him. He was to learn by experience and trusting the Holy Spirit to give him the wisdom he needed. He soon learned the people didn't believe in the baptism in the Holy Spirit with the accompanying physical evidence of speaking in tongues. According to Southern Baptist doctrine, they believed the gifts of the Holy Spirit passed away when the last apostles died. Prayer for healing was petitioned with the words, "If it be thy will." The Baptists are established in the fundamental doctrines of the new birth, water baptism, evangelism, and discipleship. Gordon made the decision to faithfully preach the Word of God, love the people, and rely on the Holy Spirit to open the eyes of their understanding to the full gospel message. Many of the church members loved the Lord and had a knowledge of the Word of God as far as they had been taught.

The following months were not without spiritual warfare. Traditionally, Baptist deacons run the church. But Gordon determined to allow the Holy Spirit to be in charge. God gave him boldness, accompanied with wisdom and love. At the end of six months, as was the custom of the church, they had a vote of confidence as to whether they wanted Gordon to continue as their pastor. People seemed to come out of the woodwork to vote against us. All the kinfolk who were members came that Sunday, although not regular church goers. They voted after the morning service. We had to leave and await our fate. The Lord doesn't need many to get His will done in the earth. He had His way, and Gordon was voted to stay on by just one vote. God is in the majority and His will prevails. Praise the Lord!

We had a big, sweet surprise in the fall of that year. We were expecting another child, and we were absolutely thrilled—especially with the possibility our third child might be a girl. Our beautiful daughter, delivered by cesarean-section, was born on June 15, 1970, in Georgia Baptist Hospital in downtown Atlanta, just blocks from Ebenezer Baptist Church, where Dr. Martin Luther King Jr. had been the pastor and where he is buried.

Zoe Elizabeth looked like a little Georgia peach. Jason and Russell were delighted to have a little sister. The ladies in the church were there to help me when I returned home, providing dinners, washing clothes, and cleaning the house.

I was asked to help teach the women's Sunday school class on Sunday mornings. The adult men had their own class, and never were the two classes to mix—women were forbidden to teach men. I knew this invitation was an ideal opportunity to teach the Word, and it caused me to sharpen my skills. I allowed the Holy Spirit to teach and enlighten the women in the truth of the baptism in the Holy Spirit and healing. I began to "cut my teeth", as it were, as I taught the Word of God in these classes. The teaching gift within me was being developed.

Betty, one of the deacon's wives, who also taught the ladies' class, was teaching from Acts 2 one Sunday morning. She suddenly asked me if I spoke another language. I was so tempted to tell her and the class that I was a tongue-talking believer, but I knew she meant had I learned to speak a known language. Of course, I answered "no" as the timing was not suitable to tell the class I often prayed in an unknown language.

Betty's husband, known as W.M., became quite vocal one evening during a mid-week service. He shouted out in the midst of Gordon's preaching,

"Preacher White, you're not going to turn this church into a *holy roller* church!"

The word was out—Gordon was a tongue-talking pastor! Fear griped W.M. as he vocalized his objection in no uncertain terms.

Gordon, a Brit, was not familiar with the term *holy roller*. He was soon to understand its meaning – an Americanism for those who were labeled Pentecostal and spoke in tongues. But W.M. soon learned that Jesus is Lord and head of the church, and the Holy Spirit was having His way.

It was exciting to see the Lord open the hearts of a few of the ladies in the church. One afternoon as I visited one of the deacon's wives, we were to experience our first real breakthrough. Trellis Gunnells, wife of J.W., chairman of the board of deacons, and I went next door to visit her sister-in-law, Maxine Parker. The subject of the baptism in the Holy Spirit came up, and they indicated their desire to receive. I laid hands on them and prayed, and they both began speaking in other tongues. The power of God was so real and tangible in the room that day, I was unable to drive home for a good while. The glory and presence of the Lord was precious. I could hardly wait to get home and tell Gordon what had happened. Well, news of what happened that afternoon spread like wild fire in the community, and other ladies got hungry. Others were upset, or you could say, angry.

It was the beginning of a transforming work of the Holy Spirit in this traditional, denominational church. It reminded me of Lydia in the book of Acts of whom it is said, "... whose heart the Lord opened, that she attended unto the things which were spoken of Paul" (Acts 16:14).

Pulling Up, Tearing Down, and Revival

How can they hear and understand without a preacher? We counted it a great privilege that God had sent us all the way from England via Canada, to bring these precious believers into the revelation of the full gospel.

Other ladies came to our home or called us to come and minister to them the baptism in the Holy Spirit. Our days were filled with joy and peace as we witnessed a Holy Spirit revival. For a season we had seven prayer meetings a week in the church – that is how hungry the people were.

"Preacher, could you meet me at the church educational building right away?" inquired the anxious voice at the other end of the phone. It was 7 a.m. on a Monday morning. Deacon W.M. Mask sounded distressed, so Gordon quickly agreed to meet him there. At first Gordon wondered if something had happened to his son as he was serving in the military in Vietnam.

"W.M. what can I do for you?"

He indicated he needed prayer, and as Gordon laid hands on him he suddenly fell to the floor and started rolling around. What a sight! This was the deacon who warned Gordon that he would not turn this Baptist church into a *holy roller* church, and here he was rolling all around the floor. The Holy Spirit had convinced him of the reality of the baptism; he couldn't wait to receive that morning. He came up speaking in tongues!

Just a few days prior to this, I had ministered to his wife Betty in the ladies Sunday School class. She had opened up and said she was ready to receive the baptism in the Holy Spirit. When she went home, the transformation in her life was so visible her husband saw the difference. He made the decision that the baptism in the Holy Spirit is real, hence the early morning phone call. W.M. became one of our strongest supporters in the church.

Christmas 1970 arrived and now several of the women were filled with the Holy Spirit. We were experiencing a New Testament revival, but not without persecution. The religious spirits were stirred, but the supernatural move of the Holy Spirit continued to prevail and spread.

It was customary for the ladies to have a special Christmas dinner in a nearby restaurant. This year would be remarkably different. Those baptized in the Holy Spirit were buzzing with excitement and giving testimonies over the Christmas dinner. Our church pianist, Sandra Roper, a sweet quiet lady, whose outward appearance displayed sadness, sat quietly listening to the testimonies and absorbing all she heard and observed. The joy of the Lord flowed out of the lives of these women she knew so well.

We all returned to our homes filled with gladness as we witnessed the move of the Holy Spirit. I got ready for bed when suddenly the phone rang. It was close to midnight. The voice at the other end of the line pleaded with me to come to her home right away.

"Barbara, this is Maxine Parker, I have Sandra Roper here. We need you to come and pray for her to receive the baptism in the Holy Spirit."

I got dressed and drove up the road at this late hour to be met by a spiritually hungry woman. Sandra had always been faithful in her music ministry and in church attendance with her two daughters, Andrea and Nena. At that time her husband was not living for the Lord. After some brief instructions on how to receive the baptism in the Holy Spirit, I laid hands on her, and immediately she began to speak in tongues. Then the Lord led me to prophesy over her. The words brought great comfort and encouragement to her heart. About an hour later she returned home exuberant in the spirit.

Sandra did something quite bold when she got home. She woke her ungodly husband Hayward and told him what had happened. He moaned and groaned but heard what she said then went back to sleep. Sandra's whole life was so transformed and the love of God flowed out of her like he had never seen before. He couldn't quite make out what had happened. He decided he wasn't going to live with a "tongue-talking" wife. His plan was to leave Sandra and the girls after Christmas. But God had another plan.

Christmas Eve arrived, and the community was still buzzing with news of what was going on in the church. It was close to midnight, and our phone rang. We became accustomed to these midnight calls.

"Preacher, could you come up and pray for Hayward? He's pacing the floor, and we don't know what to do," the voice of Sandra's mother pleaded.

Vesta was one of the ladies who had been baptized in the Holy Spirit, so she began praying in the Spirit for her family. Gordon quickly left to see what was going on with Hayward; he knew God was dealing with him. Hayward had a reputation for drinking heavily at times, even becoming involved in car accidents.

Gordon walked into the house and asked him, "What's wrong Hayward?"

He replied in a melancholy voice, "I don't know."

Gordon told him to kneel down and then led him in a prayer of salvation. As soon as Hayward had finished asking the Lord Jesus into his life, Gordon laid his hands on his head and commanded in the Name of Jesus that the spirit of alcohol leave him. He rose up on his feet, and when Gordon asked him what had happened, he replied with these words,

"I felt that spirit leave me, first going from my feet right up and out of the top of my head."

Hayward was saved and set free, praise God! Not long afterward, he was baptized in the Holy Spirit and called to preach.

Hayward and Sandra Roper eventually pastored a church in the area, and continued to serve the Lord for many years.

At the time of this writing, Hayward and Sandra are both in heaven. They are such trophies of God's grace.

I want to insert here the testimony of their daughter, Nena Roper Littlejohn. It will thrill your heart as you read this powerful testimony of what God did in their family.

Nena Roper Littlejohn

This is the place and time that my sweet Daddy gave his heart completely over to the Lord. I remember Pastor Gordon coming to our little house on Christmas Eve. My Dad was drunk and miserable. He had my grandmother call the pastor to come over and pray. That little house was filled with much joy and rejoicing as Dad poured the liquor down the drain after asking Jesus Christ to rule and reign in his life. My sister and I could hear rejoicing going on from our bedroom. We weren't sure what had happened since it was so late in the night. However, from that day forward, great changes began to take place in the Roper family.

The musical talent that both my mom and dad had was stirred up. As we attended Stewart Baptist Church and began to learn about Jesus, my dad began training my sister and me in music. Our home became a house of gospel music worship, and we began to travel to churches as The Roper Family. As the old gospel song goes, "Daddy sang bass and Momma sang tenor." Andrea and I joined right in with me singing soprano and she alto.

Pastor Gordon and Barbara White have influenced five generations for Jesus; my grandmother; my dad and mom; we their children Andrea, Nena, and Boyd; and the grandchildren Joshua and Annalise. My son, Joshua, has two girls who are growing up as worshippers and followers of Jesus – five generations!

Thank you for your obedience to come to the United States! My path would be very different if obedience hadn't been chosen. Much love to you, Gordon and Barbara.

One of the many trophies of God's grace in the church was a young man, Keith Stuarte, brother of Sandra Roper. His dear mother, Vesta, faithfully prayed for him. Her faith brought results that were to be ongoing. Keith was a young teenager whose life seemed to be going nowhere. He was affected by the early death of his father and sought consolation in drink and drugs. His appearance was that of a country hippie, but one day the Lord got hold of this young man. Gordon led him to the Lord, and he was soon baptized in the Holy Spirit. He was so keen and zealous for the Lord that he wanted to hang around Gordon and learn more of the Word of God. Soon Gordon asked him to lead the youth meetings every Monday night. One night. our daughter, Zoe, at the age of five, went forward in the youth meeting, and Keith led her to the Lord. Already fruit was coming forth in his life.

Keith attended Bible School where he met his lovely wife Rosemary. God called them into pastoral ministry. Today they are pastors of a successful church in Waterbury, Connecticut. It has been our privilege to minister in their church from time to time. What a delight to see the fruit that has come forth in Keith's life and ministry.

Gordon and I had the opportunity of ministering in a church Keith pastored in South Carolina in 1994. Out of the ministry came this wonderful testimony from one of his members:

Rhoda Wichser

> I have never forgotten the day you and your wonderful husband ministered to me and especially the *way* you two ministered together. One would speak a message in tongues, and the other

would interpret, not only by the spirit but whatever gesture, dance, laugh, clap, and so on, would be repeated in the interpretation as well.

I have since asked the Lord for a husband and ministry where my husband and I work as a team, or should I say "as one," like God used you two to minister to me and so many others. It was so delightful, so encouraging, and so much love and joy to see the way the Holy Spirit flowed through you two. I see God is still using you mightily to encourage others even through the heart's hardest pain. May our Father continue to pour through you, and may His healing virtue continue to touch you.

In 1973, Gordon was asked to serve on the Executive Board of the Billy Graham Evangelistic Association for the Atlanta Crusade. It was a joy and privilege for Gordon to support this great evangelistic outreach and to sit on the platform with many other ministers. One important dignitary attending these meetings was Governor Jimmy Carter, who was later to become the thirty-ninth President of the United States.

It was in the same year that the Lord led Gordon to contact Kenneth E. Hagin to invite him to hold meetings in Atlanta. Soon Gordon received a telephone call from Norvel Hayes, asking him to help Kenneth Hagin set up these meetings. It was Brother Hagin's first ministry visit to the city. Gordon searched for a suitable venue and finally found the East Point Civic Center. Kenneth Hagin Jr. and Buddy Harrison both helped in the meetings; Buddy led the praise and worship, and Kenneth Jr. and his wife Lynette worked the book table. Although the numbers were not large, God moved by His Spirit. The rich teaching of the Word brought revelation, and out of these meetings, others were birthed into ministry and much fruit came forth.

It was a joy to invite anointed speakers to the church who could bless the people, such as Norvel Hayes, Dr. Joe Poppell, Don Hughes, Don O'Don, and Reverend Finis Jennings Dake, the author of *Dake's Annotated Reference Bible*, plus other full gospel ministers. Gordon invited those he was led by the Lord to invite. As you know, Baptist churches are controlled by the deacons. But in this case, Gordon allowed the Holy Spirit to direct him in his decisions in shepherding the flock of God. Not all the deacons in our church embraced the baptism in the Holy Spirit and healing for today.

When Reverend Finis Jennings Dake came to minister, we were amazed he never brought a Bible. He was a walking Bible who had the supernatural ability to teach on end-time prophetic topics from Daniel and Revelation with no Bible or notes.

One day Gordon was visiting Finis at his ministry office in Lawrenceville, Georgia, when news came that Finis' son was seriously injured in a motor cycle accident. His neck was broken, and Finis asked Gordon to pray for him. The Lord graciously answered his prayer, and his son was healed and restored – praise God!

We recall one time being somewhat discouraged, which is not uncommon in ministry. We heard that Lester Sumrall was ministering in Atlanta, and we drove up to attend his meetings. Lester was a mighty man of God who flowed in the gifts of the Spirit. He prayed for us and kept speaking by the Spirit into Gordon's life these words, "Lord hold him, Lord hold him ..." We knew exactly what the Lord meant and determined to stay the course at the church. So often we must encourage ourselves in the Lord and not let His Word slip from us. Perseverance is vital in our lives to walk in faith and victory. A couple of years later Lester would be a guest in our home when we lived in Stone Mountain, Georgia.

Our ministry at Stewart Baptist Church was not without persecution as you can imagine. Those who refused to accept the truth of the full gospel left the church. Others spoke against the work of the Holy Spirit, and even threats were received on the phone to leave town by midnight. We just kept on being faithful to the Word and our God-given assignment in that place. The Lord supernaturally protected us.

Pulling Up, Tearing Down, and Revival

On one occasion Gordon was driving down the road, and gun shots rang past his car. Was someone trying to kill him? We sensed divine protection. I remember on another occasion Gordon was visiting the town of Monroe. He was shocked to discover a car was following him. He quickly found a place to park near the center of town where the parking was angle style. The car following him pulled directly behind him and blocked him in. An agitated woman stepped out and shouted, "I thought you were Charlie; I almost shot you!" Then she quickly drove off. Whoever Charlie was we'll never know. How we praised God for protecting Gordon that day.

I was involved in helping with the Women's Missionary Union in the church and before long was asked to be the program chairman. That was the green light for me to invite speakers in who were baptized in the Holy Spirit. God used different women to minister into the lives of the ladies.

In 1974, I read in a Christian magazine of the work of Women's Aglow International, a Spirit-filled women's organization based in Seattle, Washington. I contacted the leaders in the Atlanta area and found out how to start a chapter in Covington, Georgia. I gathered many of my now Spirit-filled friends together, including those from other churches, and we sought to organize a Women's Aglow Chapter. I kept wondering who would be chosen to lead. To my amazement, the leader from Atlanta, Pat Carver, felt led by the Lord to choose me. I was a little stunned, but then began to see myself called to serve in this position. After all, the Lord had given me the vision, and I humbly accepted, not knowing the full implications and responsibility.

It was an exciting venture as I began to organize, locate a suitable venue, and appoint those who would serve with me on the board. The Holy Spirit, along with Pat's capable training, enabled us to begin our first meeting in Covington in January, 1975 at Oxford College. From there we met at the First Presbyterian Church in Covington, a church whose former pastor was the famous Scottish preacher, Reverend Peter Marshall. He went on to Washington, DC, to serve twice as Chaplain of the United States Senate.

Reverend Tom White, pastor of the First Presbyterian Church at that time, graciously opened his church for us to hold Women's Aglow meetings. He became a real friend to Gordon and me. He had an unusual background, having been raised in the George Whitfield Bethesda Orphanage in Savannah, Georgia. He never knew his parents and even named himself. Through God's grace and calling on his life, he rose from extreme poverty to become a successful pastor.

Women attended the Women's Aglow meetings from different denominational backgrounds. Many were saved, healed, and baptized in the Holy Spirit. Among the speakers I hosted were Reverend Norvel Hayes, Mrs. Freda Lindsay of Christ For the Nations, Rachel Jeffries, and Gwen Shaw.

The following year, I was appointed the Women's Aglow Georgia outreach director, to assist in the formation of new chapters. Each responsibility was further training and experience for what was to come years later. To my surprise, I was appointed Georgia area president and finally a regional director, responsible for not only Georgia, but also South Carolina and Florida. My duties were to train the leadership and set up regional conventions. I met precious women of God who spoke into my life. Speaking invitations came from Tennessee and Alabama as well.

The four years I served with Women's Aglow were not without its challenges. As it was a charismatic women's organization, many different streams of teaching abounded, although most agreed on the basic full gospel teaching as laid down in their doctrinal statement. Unfortunately, some in leadership did not have a personal revelation of the *word of faith*, which is another term used by Paul to describe the full Gospel of the Lord Jesus Christ.

On one visit to the annual meeting of the regional directors in Everett, Washington, I was summoned to be questioned on my doctrinal beliefs. Reverend Dennis Bennett, of the Charismatic Episcopal stream, was so gracious to me. He stood for what the Bible declares concerning the *word of faith*, and he had a great respect for Rev. Kenneth Hagin, telling the leaders not to over-react.

Another well-known minister was not so gracious and sternly warned me that, *God was going to put his bulldozer on me for teaching faith,* accusing me of being, *an arrogant young woman.* How absurd! Knowing the truth and experiencing it for myself, I made the decision to walk in love, but at the same time rejected such condemnation. How vital to have a personal revelation of Bible faith and to walk and live in obedience to the Word of God in order to please the Lord (Hebrews 11:6).

By the time 1975 arrived, Gordon had not been home to visit his mother and family for seven years. It was an answer to prayer when the church told us they would be paying for all of us to return to Canada, England, and Wales to visit our families during the summer of 1975. How excited we were! We began our trip by driving up to Toronto to visit my family and then flying on to London. We spent a month in South Wales where Gordon's mother resided. The children loved this time with their Welsh and English cousins. It happened to be a warm, dry summer filled with many blessings from the Lord. Our vacation lasted eight weeks. Only the Lord could have arranged such a glorious trip for us as a family.

We made the decision early in our marriage to make Jesus our healer and trust Him for our health. We prayed for the children, and healing came. But much more than that, through exercising faith in His Word, we were spared from so much sickness. We are not against going to the doctor, but it is far better not to have to go.

In the process of learning the walk of faith, we decided to throw away all our over-the-counter medicine because we thought that by not taking medicine, it showed the Lord we were in faith. This was lack of understanding, and we were quick to realize that is not the way faith works. It is not because you don't take medicine that God heals. It is by believing and acting on His Word that brings results, even though you may need to take medicine as well. We were still learning and had to replace what we had thrown away to be practical.

Zoe had been experiencing ear aches as a little girl, and we found out when she had a check-up that she had some loss of hearing in one ear. We set ourselves to believe for God to restore her hearing. She gave her own testimony at age eight:

> Just before I started first grade, my mom took me to school for a hearing and sight test. The test showed I could not hear too well in one ear. We were asked to go for another test, and they told us the same thing. They asked my mom to take me to a doctor and find out what was wrong with my hearing. Ever since I was born, my parents have always taught me Jesus is our healer and that He would not only heal me but keep me healthy and

well. This time they prayed for me and believed that my ear was healed (Mark 11:23-24).

When I started third grade, the same test was given, and it showed I still could not hear perfectly in that ear, but we knew that God's Word was true and believed that Jesus had healed me. I had no pain and heard everything just fine. We continued to believe God's Word and counted it done. A few months ago, we moved to a new school, and the school gave me the same test again. This time I passed the test, and when I brought the paper home to show my mom and dad, we all praised the Lord together because He had healed me by His Word. The test at school proved and confirmed it. I know Jesus heals and keeps me well.

Chapter 11

Launching Out into the Deep

During the summer of 1976, our ministry at Stewart Baptist Church drew to a close. We knew we had completed our assignment. God had done so many miracles and shown Himself strong on our behalf, graciously bringing many into the fullness of the Spirit and revelation of His Word with manifestations of healing and miracles. In fact, the whole of Newton County was affected by the power of God. People from different denominational churches came to the meetings and received multiplied blessings through the ministry of the Holy Spirit. We indeed had a revival in the real sense of the word, not just a week of special meetings each summer, but an ongoing move of the Spirit of God, liberating the captives and enlightening the believers.

In the meetings, we allowed the gifts of the Spirit to flow. At that time, I flowed in the gift of tongues, and Gordon ministered the interpretation of tongues. Gordon took the liberty to invite Spirit-filled speakers to minister, much to the dismay of the deacons. No pastor had ever done such a thing. We even had an African-American preacher come to minister, the Director of Teen Challenge in Georgia. It was the first time an African-American minister preached there in the church's history. The boldness God gave us enabled us to cut across the religious and cultural racism that prevailed in the southern United States at that time.

The Lord was leading us on to the next phase of our ministry during the summer of 1976. A door opened in Stone Mountain, Georgia, for Gordon to serve as co-pastor with Pastor Doug Chatham of Our Shepherds Church, a charismatic Baptist church. We looked forward to moving to the city and found a suitable house to rent in Decatur. The children enrolled in Our Shepherd's Academy, and we made many lasting friendships there.

Our Shepherd's Church had a vision to start satellite churches, one of which was in Rex, Georgia. Gordon faithfully ministered at this new church plant, and I taught the women's weekly Bible studies. This continued for a year. People were hungry so it was easy to minister the Word of God, confirmed by signs following. It was during this season God began to use Gordon in praying specifically for those with back problems, and the Lord lengthened legs on a regular basis.

At the end of the year, Gordon was asked to be the full-time pastor of the Rex church, but he didn't feel it was in the Lord's plan. Instead, a young enthusiastic couple, Paul and

Nancy Glass, were invited to preach one Sunday, and they felt they should be the pastors, much to our delight and those of the congregation. They have continued to faithfully pastor there with much fruit and many blessings. Paul and Nancy are very special friends, and we have continued to enjoy rich fellowship with them over the years.

Our season at Our Shepherds was short lived, but God used Gordon in the healing ministry with many receiving miracles from the Lord. When we left the church, God opened doors for us to minister in other churches, and soon after we started our own ministry. We held meetings in Stone Mountain under the name Prevailing Word Fellowship. We also ministered in Georgia and Florida as God opened the doors. We were invited for guest appearances on television in South Carolina, Channel 40 (CBN) in Atlanta, and in Ft. Lauderdale, Florida.

We began an outreach by writing a teaching magazine, *The Prevailing Word*, which was sent throughout the United States and other nations. We had no idea God would release us to the nations within a few years. Looking back, we see how God enlarged our vision.

My mother, Beulah Newcomb, visited us from Canada during the Christmas holiday in 1978. The Lord gave her a miracle in her body. She shares her testimony:

> While attending services in Stone Mountain, Georgia where my son in law Gordon White

pastors, I received a wonderful healing. One of my legs was shorter than the other, and when Gordon prayed for me, I felt my leg lengthen. It was witnessed by others. To God be the glory! By His stripes we were healed. With man it was impossible, but with God all things are possible. Thank you, Jesus!

One dear couple we were able to encourage in ministry during our Atlanta days was Lucius and Ethel Edmondson. Lucius directed a successful ministry called Team Jesus, a ministry to the motorcycle people. He and Ethel have had tremendous success in evangelism and leading people into the baptism in the Holy Spirit. Today Lucius is Chaplain for two prisons in the Atlanta area and is involved in training others in the prison ministry. Team Jesus is still flourishing.

We met a beautiful and energetic young lady at Our Shepherds Church. Sheryl Thomas, whose heart was to serve, offered to help in our ministry and blessed us with administrative skills, bookkeeping and music. Helping care for our children when needed brought her joy. Gordon was privileged to assist her father-in-law in performing her marriage to Timothy Grey in June of 1979. Our three children were included in the bridal party.

I was still involved in Women's Aglow and continued to speak at various chapters and retreats in the southeast as the

Lord opened doors. I ministered in other churches, too. One such meeting was at a Methodist church in Lithonia, Georgia. One of the ladies attending, a Mrs. Clelland, was baptized in the Holy Spirit that day. I later found out she is the mother of Max Clelland who was the Veterans Secretary under President Jimmy Carter's administration.

You just never know whom the Lord will lead you to minister to. On another occasion as I was speaking at a women's meeting in Carrollton, Georgia, a dear woman asked me to pray for her. She was Mrs. Jackie Gingrich, and she too was baptized in the Holy Spirit; she was the first wife of Newt Gingrich.

In 1979, Gordon published his first book, *What On Earth Are you Saying?* with editorial help from Elise Whitworth. Since then, this book has been translated into French, Urdu, and Dutch.

Gordon had a great love and appreciation for the ministry and life of Smith Wigglesworth of Bradford, Yorkshire, England. His life of faith is such an inspiration to believers. Gordon asked his nephew, Paul Croft, a ministry associate in London, to go to Bradford and see if he could find the house where Wigglesworth had lived, or gain any information on his life. The Lord led Paul to the home of Olive Wigglesworth, the daughter-in-law of Smith, who was eighty-nine years of age at the time. She took quite a liking to Paul and openly shared with him Smith's life and ministry. We quote the report Paul sent us in 1979:

> I would like to share with you an experience I had recently during a visit to Bradford, Yorkshire while seeking information on the world famous early twentieth-century evangelist Smith Wigglesworth. I was surprised to find a general lack of information about this great man of God. However, the Lord directed me to the home of Olive Wigglesworth, aged eighty-six years, widow of Smith Wigglesworth's son Harold.
>
> She lived just a hundred yards from the house in which Smith lived and had his plumbing workshop. This very dear Christian lady welcomed me warmly and was happy to share her treasured memories of her father-in-law, or "Granddad,", as she used to call him.
>
> Olive vividly recalled healings within his ministry, and testified to healings that took place within the family. She said that when he laid hands upon you, it felt as though you were on fire. Many times it seemed as though Smith was

on fire himself when he preached, often taking off his coat and rolling up his shirt sleeves.

Olive was quick to stress that "Granddad" always gave God the glory and never claimed any glory for himself. The more she spoke about Smith Wigglesworth, the more she seemed to glow with the excitement of just knowing him. The fact that she knitted all his socks was a privilege she greatly cherished. Just sharing an hour with this dear lady was a blessing indeed from the Lord.

But the measure of her generosity and love was truly displayed when she insisted I take one of her cherished photographs of Smith and a New Testament of his, which he had given to her as a present. This New Testament has many passages of Scripture marked and underlined with notes and comments by Smith. I feel privileged to have it in my possession.

When Paul visited us in January 1980 he brought the New Testament with him to show us. Kenneth Hagin, upon hearing that Paul had the New Testament, flew Gordon and Paul to Tulsa to meet with him as he wanted to see Smith's

New Testament. Brother Hagin photo copied it with all the personal markings and notes. Later on Paul was led to give it to Harrison House library of ministry memorabilia so that others could see it. Paul's sister, Sylvia, who resided in Bradford at the time, eventually found Smith's home where he conducted his plumbing business before going into ministry. We have photos of his home on file in our office.

At the end of 1977 I completed my ministry responsibilities with Women's Aglow. It was time to move on in the direction I was receiving from the Lord. I started Faith Women of America, an outreach of our ministry, holding local Bible studies. I thought it would be good to put on a conference in Atlanta during the summer of 1980. Other women and ministries offered to help and support these meetings. We found an excellent venue at a college in Carrollton, Georgia. As we prayed and sought the Lord, something just didn't seem to set well in our spirits, and we cancelled the meetings. I was a little disappointed for a time, but I did not lose the vision and held it in my heart. It just wasn't the right time or place to set up these women's meetings. I committed it to the Lord and knew He would show me what to do in the future. My vision was limited to Georgia, but God's plan was far bigger and better than what I had originally planned. How it pays to be led of the Holy Spirit.

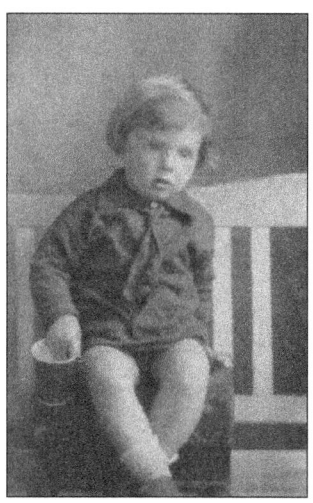

Young Gordon three years old in Wales

Baby Barbara 1940 Canada

Gordon early childhood in Wales

Mom, Barbara, and sister Betty, 1945, New Brunswick, Canada

Teenage Gordon in London

Barbara's Family Fort St. John, British Columbia 1948

Ruth Grantham, Betty, and Barbara, Winter in Toronto 1959

Gordon in his twenties

Gordon's first faith car

Engaged at Christmas 1963

Gordon preaching in Trafalgar Square, London May 1964

In love in London. 1964

Our Wedding Day August 19, 1964

Gordon and Barbara Newlyweds, Worthing, Sussex

Gordon preaching, London Revival Crusade 1964

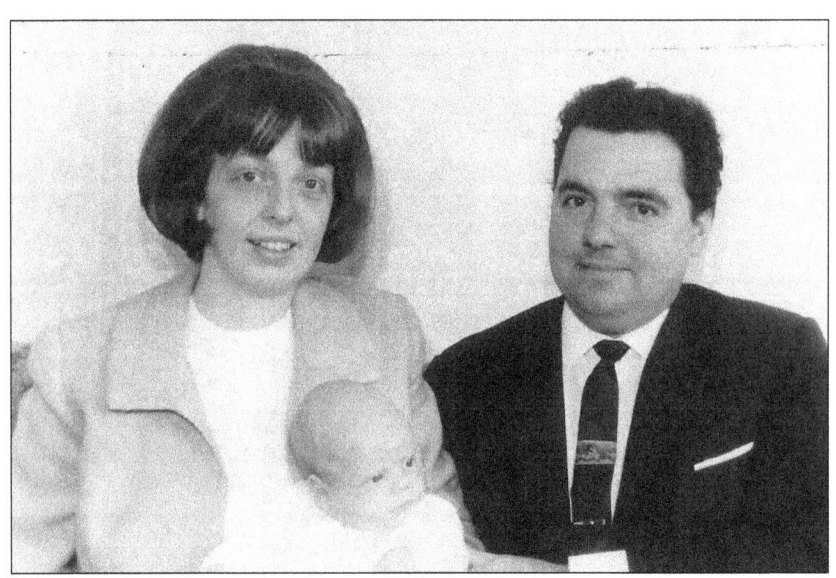

Happy young parents 1966

Gordon preaching at Stewart Baptist Church, Covington, Georgia in the 1970's

Jason and Russell playing at the parsonage, Covington, Georgia

Jason, Russell, and Zoe Christmas 1972

Family Vacation in Florida 1972

Proud Daddy of three

July 4 family picnic at Stone Mountain, Georgia

Ministering on TV in Fort Lauderdale, Florida 1977

Beginning of our international ministry London 1989

First Ministry in Paris, France 1990

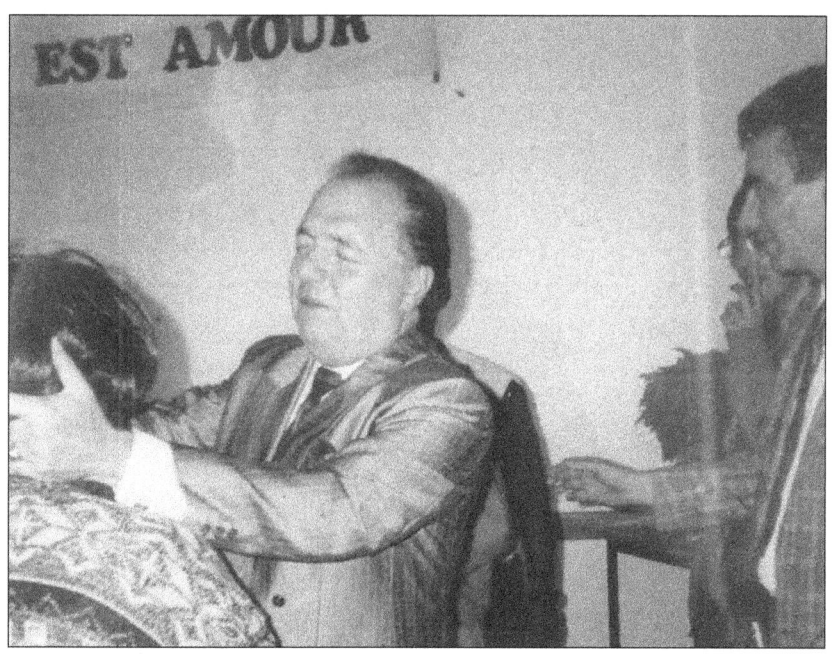

Gordon ministering for Pastor Marc Lebrun in Paris, France

First ministry in Belgium with Maria Rossi our translator, 1991

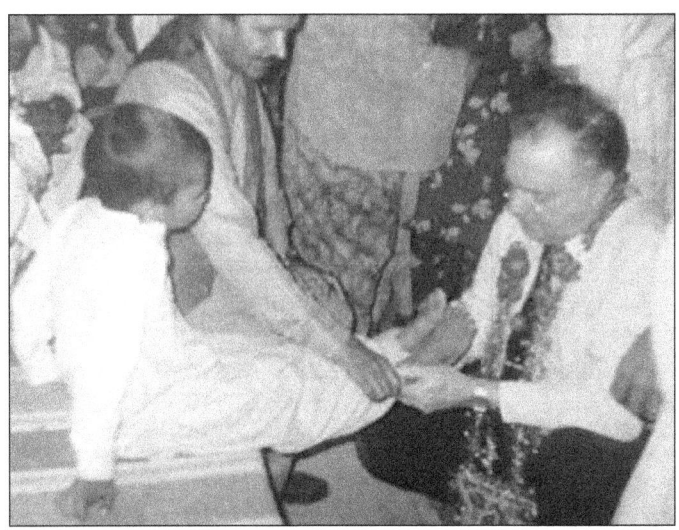

Gordon ministering God's healing power in Pakistan November 1990

Pastors who hosted us in Pakistan

Barbara preaching in Pakistan crusade 1990

Barbara ministering to the women in Pakistan 1990

Ministry in Nigeria 1990's

Ministering on Television in Bermuda 1992

Gordon on the Sea of Galilee, Israel 1998

Faith Women International meeting in Bermuda
Barb Witt, Mieke Colleé, Maria Rossi, and Barbara 1999

Happy Memories with Papa, Nana, and seven grandkids

Alaska Cruise 2003

Celebrating our 40th Wedding Anniversary with Pastor's Keith and Rosemary Stuarte Waterbury, Connecticut 2004

Our 40th Wedding Anniversary at the Mission Inn, Riverside, California

Our 43rd Wedding Anniversary in San Clemente, California 2007

Chapter 12

Westward Bound
— California Years

We were invited to minister in a meeting in East Point, Georgia, in May of 1979. A lady prophesied over Gordon words to the effect that "we were to prepare ourselves as we would be going from the east to the west, from the west to the east, and back to the west, and would bring a mighty deliverance to the people."

Not fully perceiving what the Lord was saying, we sought Him to confirm these words and give us understanding. Previously, the Lord spoke to Gordon that he would be going to California to minister. Was this the time?

An opportunity opened for us to go to California during the month of August in 1979. I was invited to attend a "Women of The Word" conference held at Redlands University hosted by Rachel Jeffries. We had a witness that we should drive to California and believe that other doors would open for ministry while there. It was a God-ordained trip. The children enjoyed travelling across the states, and especially arriving in California – a complete change from the south-east. We were amazed at the beauty of the desert, magnificent mountains, the Pacific Ocean, and the expansive Los Angeles metropolis. Pastors Bob and Rachel Jeffries graciously hosted us in their home.

Sure enough, the Lord opened doors to minister in several churches and meetings, the first of which was at Pass Christian Center in Banning. Other churches included Irvine and Azusa. We spent a few days in the San Diego area and ministered at a church in Mira Mar. I spoke to ladies groups in both Mira Mar and Irvine. Each meeting was accompanied by testimonies of God's healing power.

One day we took a side trip into Tijuana, our first visit to Mexico. At the end of the month we travelled back to Georgia via Las Vegas, the Grand Canyon, Oklahoma City, Tulsa, and St. Louis, in time to get the children back to school. We pondered the prophetic words "east to west and west to east" and prayed about the prophetic word we had received. As I write, I have a clearer understanding of these prophetic words. I believe it included going from Georgia to California, California back to Georgia, and ultimately moving to California. However, I believe the full meaning was going to Europe in 1989 and back home to California in 2000.

Within eighteen months, March 1981, we were packed and prepared for the long move west to California. Gordon received an invitation to pastor, and when we prayed, it seemed good to the Lord and us to take this pastoral position. Where were we going? To the church in Banning where we had visited with Pastors Bob and Rachel Jeffries on our first visit to California. The church, located in what is called "The Pass" in the city of Banning, is situated between the highest mountains in southern California. San Jacinto and San Gorgonio make for a picturesque location. Banning was a resort town many years earlier, a stopover for the movie stars en route from Hollywood to Palm Springs. The almond and peach industry had flourished there in years gone by.

Gordon, along with our boys, drove the u-haul with our furniture and car in tow. I flew to Palm Springs with Zoe and our little dog Cuddles via Los Angles, thanks to the generosity of a brother in the Lord, Mr. Coffie, of Detroit, Michigan. In fact, the cost of the whole move was financed by this brother. We were used to faith adventures and were always excited to step out in obedience to the Lord's directions. God had used Mr. Coffie to allow us to live in his home in Stone Mountain for nearly two years. God has unlimited ways of providing for His children.

It is a blessing not to know everything about the future. The culture of this small California town differed significantly from the southern hospitality and pace of Georgia. The first few hours there gave us an indication that this town was somewhat different – the tow bar attached to the U-Haul was stolen in broad daylight, minutes after our arrival. Someone visiting us thought it strange there were so many police cars for the size of the town. That in itself spelled crime. We experienced further thefts, our sons' bicycles were stolen, and rocks were thrown through one of the front windows of the parsonage. Since the church was located close to the freeway, we had strange visitors from time to time, looking for help. Often on a Saturday night, there would be fighting and other disturbances in the house next door, robbing us of the rest we needed for ministry on Sunday. But we chose to be happy, serving the Lord.

Our home was the little white parsonage located literally a few yards adjacent to the church. We squeezed our furniture into our new home and carried on with the Lord's work with joy and appreciation for all His goodness. It wasn't long before we found ourselves in many good "fights of faith."

In fact, many opportunities awaited us to engage in intense intercession for this area. The history and founding of the church was not laid on a sound foundation, and strife within the church often tried to rear its ugly head. Without the Lord's grace and wisdom, we would not have survived the stress and opposition that came against the Word of God and us. The pressures began to affect Gordon's health, but we stood fast on the Word, knowing no weapon formed against us could successfully prosper. There was an onslaught of demon activity in the town, likened to Nazareth, where Jesus could not do much due to the unbelief of the people. It is one thing to preach the Gospel, but another thing for the people to receive the Word and act upon what they hear.

We endeavored to faithfully preach and teach the Word to the people and shepherd the flock God entrusted to us. Somehow we knew God was at work in us and through us, even though the way was more than a little uncomfortable. In fact, it was dreadfully stressful at times, but we determined to stay the course and be faithful until the Lord said "Move on". In times like these, the Word and the Holy Spirit builds strength within the believer and makes one like David said:

> Your God has commanded your strength [your might in His service, and impenetrable hardness to temptation]; O God, display Your might and strengthen what You have wrought for us! (Psalm 68:28 AMP)

Was God preparing us for the future? Were there plans for us beyond this little town? To be honest, our vision went beyond the boundaries of Banning, but we were prepared to be faithful until such a time when He would release us.

While we pastored in Banning, the Lord started using us in the prophetic gifts of the Holy Spirit. Gordon ministered in the gift of tongues, and I would always have the interpretation. It was an edifying word for the person or even groups of people.

The word of wisdom and word of knowledge often flowed through the prophetic utterances. We continued to develop ourselves in these gifts and allowed the Holy Spirit to minister through us. Each time people were lifted up, given courage, and hope was released for their particular situation. We taught the recipients the importance of the prophetic word and how to pray over the prophecy and hold fast to what God had spoken to them – to war a good warfare in faith and see the fulfillment of the promises come to pass (1 Timothy 1:19).

Our oldest son, Jason, worked on a local peach farm one summer. He stepped on a nail, and a serious infection developed in his foot. We prayed and nothing happened, other than his foot got worse, so to the hospital we took him to be treated. The doctor didn't give us a positive report. He even said Jason probably would have to have his foot amputated. Knowing what the Word says, we quickly took authority over this condition, reversing the bad report with the words from Isaiah 54:17 (AMP):

"Every tongue [word] that shall rise against you in judgment you shall show to be in the wrong."

We told the devil he would not steal our son's foot! Sure enough, through exercising faith in His healing Word and prayer, plus an antibiotic, he fully recovered, praise God. Up to this time we had always received quick results with our children when it came to healing. In fact, this was the first time we didn't see healing manifest like at other times. The Lord showed us the time comes when children, who are trained in the Word of God, are old enough, they are to exercise their own faith and receive the promises of God. This of course, we shared with Jason, who was sixteen at the time. He started being responsible for his own faith walk, not that you ever stop praying for your children.

One day Gordon met a little boy getting off the school bus in front of the church in Banning. In his caring and pastoral way Gordon asked him, "Do you go to Sunday School or church?"

His reply was not at all what he expected. "Yes, I go over there to that blood pressure church!"

Gordon thought, "A church that causes blood pressure? Maybe so! My own church here in Banning isn't helping my blood pressure with all the problems I am dealing with! Churches are supposed to get people healed of blood pressure!" Then Gordon quickly identified the church the little boy was referring to – The Precious Blood Catholic Church located a few blocks away!

While in Banning the Lord opened the door for us to minister weekly on the radio, two radio stations in Riverside and one in Palm Desert. We endeavored to use every opportunity to preach the Word, in season and out of season.

We were blessed to enjoy the beautiful amenities of the area, including Palm Springs and the mountain villages of Idyllwild and Oak Glen. We even frequented a fish restaurant in Yucca Valley, situated in the high desert, where they served British style fish and chips. This is the last place on earth where one would expect to find such a restaurant. The California weather is always sunny and hot, with a short, cool, rainy season during the winter months in contrast to the wet British weather.

The Lord surrounded us with pastors who became special friends, always encouraging us in the work of the Lord. Dan and Lynn Bennett, pastors in Ontario at that time, stood with us in faith during the difficulties in Banning, and we enjoyed great fellowship together. Tom and Gayle Slayton, who are still pastors in Hemet, gave us prayerful support. How much we need each other in the Body of Christ.

Family Blessings

My sister Elizabeth and I realized that our immediate Newcomb family had not all been together at the same time for twenty-one years. We agreed it had been far too long, so she started organizing (her forte) a family reunion in Langley, British Columbia, during the month of July 1982. It all came together with much prayer and preparation. The Lord provided for our family to fly up to British Columbia to enjoy many events for this happy occasion. The reunion culminated in a large picnic in a park where many of the Newcomb clan gathered from far and near. The matriarch was our great Aunt Ivah.

"Hi Sis, this is Elden."

I was about to drop the phone but quickly recognized it was the voice of my youngest brother. "Wow, he has never phoned me before – what's up? is he okay?" Thoughts raced through my mind. It didn't take long for him to get to the point.

"Sis, I've been listening to a music cassette Mom gave me by David Ingles. The Lord has been speaking to me, and I want to get my life right with the Lord. Since the birth of our son, Christopher, I realize I need to be a good dad in order to raise him in the Lord."

"Mmm, yes of course", I said, as I gathered my thoughts. "Was this for real, what's going on, is Elden serious?

I quickly made the decision to believe what he said and proceeded to lead him in a prayer of repentance and rededication to the Lord. I knew in my spirit he absolutely meant what he prayed. He was loved and restored into fellowship with the One he had made Lord of his life as a child of eight. We rejoiced together. The prodigal son was now home and ready to partake of His Heavenly Father's bountiful table of blessings.

Within a month, his sweet wife Isabel was born again, and the blessings began to flow, including the birth of two more sons, Adam and Matthew.

The following spring, Elden, Isabel, and Christopher visited us in Banning. It was so sweet as Elden and I sang a duet during the Sunday morning service ,"In Jesus Name", a David Ingles song.

In January of 1984, we felt led by the Lord to relocate the church to the growing town of Sunnymead; later the name was changed to Moreno Valley. It was a time of refreshing, new beginnings, and relief from the pressures we had been subjected to in Banning. In the larger picture, Banning was a stepping stone to God's greater plan.

We set about to evangelize and reach out to the many families who relocated from Los Angeles and Orange County. The church grew, and the Lord sent precious people to help us. Of note are Larry and Marchet Harts. Years later, the Lord released them into full-time ministry and they are presently pastors of a church in Sterling, Illinois.

One Sunday, a young man visited the church looking for a place where he could grow in the Lord. He was stationed at March Air Force base and was awaiting the arrival of his wife, Femi, from Germany. It was obvious Cliff Lawson had a call of God on his life and was willing to help us in whatever need we had. Finally Femi arrived, and we celebrated with a shower for her and Cliff. Within a few days they were awakened by neighbors in the early hours of the morning as their apartment was on fire. They were able to climb over the balcony and be rescued but lost many of their possessions. They stayed with us for a short time until they found a new home. Cliff and Femi followed the Lord's plan and relocated to San Francisco at the end of 1989. They ministered with excellence in the pastoral work in the town of Vallejo, conducting their ministry, Wells of Blessings.

I recently received this powerful testimony from a man who attended our church in Moreno Valley when he was in his early twenties:

> I am reaching a milestone I never thought would happen; I did not plan for this. Some of my longtime friends know that I never expected to live past twenty-five. It was the eighties and I lived like the nineties would never come. Here I am turning fifty. Someone told me that God had provided forgiveness for my sins. I didn't know at the time how those words would change my life and spark me to go to church a few weeks later. It wasn't a giant church that had cool music and all the frills; it was just a small church that met at a high school. With all the prayers that I'm sure people thought were going unheard on my behalf, God chose me that day to follow Him. I was a no-good drug dealer with a $200-a-day habit that I couldn't stop no matter how hard I tried. That day I was set free from the devil drug Meth.

I want to thank Gordon and Barbara White for being faithful prayer warriors and pastoring the church that changed my life. Gordon is now with our Heavenly Father, rejoicing with so many others that have passed on. So many things have happened in my life since that day. The only thing I would tell you is God's forgiveness is free, and your regrets and sins have been paid for by the Blood of His Son on the cross. It was the best thing that has ever happened to me.

We want to share another miraculous testimony during our time in Moreno Valley.

Our Miracle Home - Christopher and Diane Crawford

Pastor Gordon White, a friend of ours in Moreno Valley, California, in the eighties, felt inspired to help us get a vision for a better home. He and his wife Barbara invited us to spend an entire day looking at model homes. We thought, 'What's the point? We're penniless!' But at the end of the day, while sitting in a beautifully furnished model home, Pastor Gordon sat with a sly smile on his face, as if he knew something we didn't. He said he wanted to inspire us to believe for something better. He wanted to make us divinely dissatisfied. If we're stuck in our dreary old surroundings, how can we be inspired?

Pastor Gordon gave us this Scripture to stand on for our home, "And my people shall dwell in a peaceable habitation, and in sure dwellings, and in quiet resting places" (Isaiah 32:18).

We didn't know until recently, from that day on, Pastor Gordon relentlessly stayed in faith with us, asking God to give us a home.

We visited an open house in the mountains, and five other people were viewing it. I said in a loud voice "I'll take it!". We had favor with our realtor, Bruce. Shortly after, we were speechless when Bruce told us he wanted to give Mr. Kawohl, the investor and owner of the property, a piece of property to be our down payment. Bruce told us "I had to, God spoke to me and told me to do it."

The investor's wife told us, "I've put a mark on your application because I want you to have the house."

Suddenly, the realtor opened a conventional escrow account in order for us to purchase the property. They leased the house to us while it was in escrow. On December 31, we received a call from the escrow company asking us to close escrow and pay the balance of $2,500. When we went to the office, in faith, but without the money, the office lady perked up and said, "Didn't you hear? The realtor paid it!" Not only did he give us the money from another piece of property as a down payment, he paid the escrow closing cost.

God wasn't finished yet. The house was full of good quality furniture, and they decided to leave it for us. God had fulfilled His covenant promise to us based on Deuteronomy 6:10-11:

> "And when the Lord your God brings you into the land which He swore to your fathers, to Abraham, Isaac, and Jacob, to give you, with great and goodly cities which you did not build. And houses full of all good things which you did not fill, and cisterns hewn out which you did not hew, and vineyards and olive trees which you did not plant..."

Chapter 13

Released to the Nations

In 1985, while pastoring the church in Moreno Valley, California, the Lord spoke to Gordon while sitting at his desk, saying He was changing his office from pastor to prophet. He confirmed it in 1988 through a prophetic word given in a church in London, England, explaining that it would be a process. *"First the ear, then the blade, and then the full corn in the ear."* (Mark 4:28).

It was a process over the years. God used hardship, experience, dedication, assimilation, and revelation of the Word. We were positioned at the right time to enter into this major change.

There was a stirring in our spirits during 1988; we really felt the Lord was releasing us from pastoral ministry and launching us into a new season. We didn't know how or when; we just continued to pray and wait on the Lord. As autumn of that year approached, we had a phone call from our dear friend, Dr. Chuck Flynn, an anointed prophet of the Lord. He and his wife, Mary Ann, had been praying for us, and the

Lord instructed them to give us the air miles they had accumulated in order for us to make a trip back to England to minister. During the summer of 1985, we had spent three weeks in England ministering in London. It was a foretaste of what was to come on the Lord's timetable.

We were surprised, but not entirely. Maybe it was the timing – or just how the Lord opened the way for us to go. By October 4th, we were on our way, excited and knowing the Lord had far more blessings planned than we knew at that moment.

Doors swung open to preach and minister in churches in London, Bristol, Bath, Bournemouth, and Ramsgate. We travelled to Wales and other places where we connected with family and old friends. We were kept busy ministering for six weeks. It just felt good in our spirits to be in England.

Yes, something was right about being there. Was the Lord positioning and preparing us for the next season on His calendar? As we drove through the beautiful English countryside, the trees were ablaze with autumn colors. We stopped at local inns for our meals and *olde worlde* tea shops to savor the delicious *cream teas*. That is just an aside – the real tug in my heart was to live in England again after leaving nineteen years earlier.

This desire was quite unusual as I had never wanted to return to England to live until that moment. I shared with Gordon what I was hearing in my spirit, and Gordon quickly dismissed it. I said nothing more for a time, but Gordon knew I was praying. We both knew the Lord was changing our office, and we would be released to a travelling ministry, but Gordon's understanding at that time was that California would be our base.

Oh, but the Lord had other plans. I don't know why I got the message first. Gordon finally caught on and agreed because of the witness in our spirits. I knew we should prepare to move back to England to set up our ministry base there. It didn't take long to position ourselves and get ready for this major move. We sold most of our furniture, packed a number of boxes, and found a good home for our dog, Cuddles. Everything was fitting into place.

Our sons were living away from home. Russell completed his education at Universal Technical Institute in Phoenix, Arizona. Jason graduated from the University of California Riverside in June of that year, and Zoe graduated from high school and was wondering what to do and where to go. She decided to move with us to England.

Just a short time before we flew to England on March 13, 1989, we received a phone call from Conrad Hall, a long time friend in England. He heard we were moving back to the London area and informed us he had two one bedroom apartments in Putney in south-west London. He could not sell them at that time and wanted us to live in them rent free. We rejoiced and accepted this supernatural provision from the Lord.

We arrived in London totally relying on the Lord for everything we would need. From the moment our feet hit the ground, door after door opened to minister in England and Wales. We settled into our new home – the two apartments in Putney were connected by a door giving us access to two living rooms, two bedrooms, two kitchens, and two bathrooms. They were located on the ground floor of a stately old Georgian home that had once been home to the curator of the famous Kew Gardens situated on the Thames River west of London. We believed and prayed for everything we needed, and the Lord faithfully provided. I made the decision to believe God for new furniture and sure enough the Lord honored my desire.

For two years we lived in these grand apartments. When Jason graduated from university, he was led by the Lord to come to England for a season. We had plenty of room for him to live with us. The Lord favored him with a job in the financial district in the city of London, working for one of the Lloyds of London companies. God gave him valuable experience. When he moved back to California the following year, his employer was quite impressed with his resume. He later went on to another company and moved into a top position in the wholesale insurance industry in Los Angeles. It is nothing other than the blessing of the Lord.

Zoe didn't fit in too well with life in England. It was a real culture shock to say the least. She lasted a total of thirty days. We knew it was in God's will for her to return to California, and we said our goodbyes and released her into the Lord's hand. She said to us, "Mom and Dad, I know God has called you to be missionaries and travel, but I know I must go back to live in California."

She returned to live with her brother, Russell, and he helped her get a job at the same company where he was working, an auto dealership in Riverside. Russell and Zoe flew over to visit us in November of 1989. The Lord began doing things for our children that we could not have done had they been with us. How sweet to trust in Jesus and allow him to look after our children.

We had special visitors in August of 1989. My sister Elizabeth, her husband John, and sons, David and Erik stopped off for a few days in London en route to Nairobi, Kenya. They were looking forward to two years mission work in that country. I had fun being tour guide around London.

One highlight was the visit to St. Paul's Cathedral and climbing the 530 steps to the top of the Whispering Gallery and the Golden Gallery where we stepped outside to take in a panoramic view of the old city of London. We also had a delightful day's visit by train down to South Wales, taking in the sights of Cardiff and Caerphilly. Gordon's sister Pearl lived in Caerphilly at that time, where the grand medieval castle called us to explore its haunting fortress.

Elizabeth and John were with us to celebrate our twenty fifth wedding anniversary on August 19. We savored a dinner together at Jack Straw's Castle Inn on Hampstead Heath in north London before ministering in a church in the area. We were sorry our children couldn't be with us to join the celebration, but we were so thankful that a few members of the family from Canada celebrated with us on this blessed occasion.

Chapter 14

Open Doors into Africa and Beyond

We went through every door the Lord opened to us in England and Wales. During the first year, it meant travelling from church to church in London and throughout the south and south-west of England and South Wales

There was plowing, sowing, and watering of the Word everywhere we went. The Lord confirmed the preaching of the Gospel with signs following as Jesus promised in Mark 16:20. Hunger prevailed in the hearts of the people. The word the Lord gave Gordon when we first started ministry in Europe was from Psalm 110:3:

> Thy people shall be willing in the day of thy power, in the beauty of holiness from the womb of the morning. (KJV)

> Your people will offer themselves willingly in the day of Your power, in the beauty of holiness. (AMP)

There is a preparation time for revival in the hearts of God's people. They must be willing and obedient to be used in the harvest field.

We purchased a used BMW car on our arrival in London. During a visit to Caerphilly in South Wales we stayed with Gordon's sister, Pearl, while ministering in various churches in the area. One day, we took a lunchtime walk into the town, and upon our return we were shocked to find our car was gone – nowhere to be found. We promptly reported it to the police and proceeded to rent a car to complete our appointments and return home to Putney. Two weeks later we were informed that the car was found abandoned in a parking lot in Cardiff, stripped and no longer drivable. We quickly replaced our car.

It was during the same visit to Wales that we ministered in a church in the town of Blackwood, not far from where Gordon was born. It was quite evident that the spiritual temperature of Wales had greatly declined from the days of the great Welsh Revival. We observed a sign at the entrance of the town boldly declaring it a "No Christian Zone." The revivalists of 1904-1905, Evan Roberts and the women who assisted him, would have been shocked. We were informed that witchcraft prevailed, hence the sign. We continue to believe God for a mighty Holy Spirit revival to sweep through the beautiful land of past revival, verdant mountains, and harmonious songs. We believe the revival fires will burn once again, and men and women will arise out of the vestiges to proclaim the glorious Gospel of the Lord Jesus Christ with mighty signs and wonders.

African Adventure

We ministered in many London churches during our first year in London, some of which were pastored by Nigerians and Ghanaians. They were so eager to hear the Word and received the ministry of the Holy Spirit with joy and gladness.

As a result of ministry in one of the London churches, we were invited to preach in Nigeria in August of 1990. As it was our first visit to the continent of Africa, we prepared ourselves in prayer and practical ways to adapt to a new country and West African culture.

We flew from London to Lagos and were greeted by a doctor from the host church in Port Harcourt. Stepping out of the airport in Lagos was more than overwhelming. There were people everywhere offering to assist us. There was no personal space. Nigeria is the most populous African country and known for its violence, causing us to watch and pray. Soon we were whisked off in a taxi to a hotel to spend one night before journeying on to Port Harcourt. Unfortunately, the five-star hotel didn't accept Nigerian naira, so we were taken in a taxi to search for another hotel. Finally, tired and overwhelmed by our new surroundings, we were escorted into a one story hotel that looked more like a prison. "Was it safe?", we wondered. We decided to make the best of our situation. It was only for one night. The smelly, dingy room had security bars on the window and the television was bolted down so as not to be stolen. The sign on the back of the door warned of HIV.

We were so sleep deprived by this time, but somehow we slept a few hours only to be awakened at dawn by the noise of the people clamoring through the streets – some going to work, others carrying goods to and from the markets in baskets precisely balanced on their heads. Happy children filled the streets on their way to school. Mothers washed clothes at the local public water pump. The sight was captivating, to say the least.

We brought bottles of water from England that kept us hydrated for awhile. Before long the doctor arrived and escorted us by taxi to a small local airport to continue our journey to Port Harcourt. In the meager airport lounge we were able to get a cup of tea and a small snack. When asked if we wanted milk in our tea, we thought we were being asked if we wanted pig's milk. Actually, it was the brand of canned milk called Peak's Milk.

It was time to board the plane for the hour's flight to our next destination. The odor on the plane indicated it had not been cleaned or sanitized for a long time. When served refreshments, we found them quite unpalatable but thanked the Lord for His provision. It was so good to finally arrive at El Shaddai Church and be warmly greeted by Pastor Elkannah Hanson and staff. We were confident of the Lord's protection, and more than that, we were in great expectation of all the wonderful things God was going to do in the meetings. The pastor asked us to preach and teach on Bible prosperity.

We were driven to our hotel to rest and prepare for the up-coming week of meetings. We were so thankful the hotel was five-star (but not by American standards), and our room was more like a suite. No sooner had we arrived, the phone rang. Gordon answered the call and began to thank the lady for offering to help in any way. I felt in my spirit it was not someone from the church, and sure enough, it turned out to be a prostitute who saw us arrive and was quick to offer her services to the foreign guest.

Each night when we arrived back at our hotel from the meetings, always escorted by people from the church, these ladies of the night were lined up ready to ply their trade. We were especially careful not to leave the hotel unescorted, or to walk down the street to one of the local markets. It was far too dangerous. We felt like we needed eyes in the back of our heads, but more than that, we knew the angels were guarding us.

The meetings were mightily blessed of the Lord. Mornings and evenings we taught and preached the Word. God used us to bring His healing, delivering power to the people. We also ministered prophetic words of encouragement and comfort to many pastors.

Angel on Assignment

While Gordon and I were ministering in these series of meetings in the church in Port Harcourt, we encountered a situation that could have caused us to panic and fear for our lives.

The long evening service concluded around eleven p.m. The hot, humid West African weather added weariness to our exhausted bodies. As we were escorted by car back to our hotel, we were suddenly apprehended by a group of city policemen along a foreboding dark road under a bridge. The police claimed one of the headlights on the car was out, but we were not certain this was so. They began shouting to the driver with intimidating threats to take us to jail. Our driver shouted back and asked, "What are you going to do, take us to jail and shoot us?" The other option was the possibility of being required to pay a bribe for our freedom. Our driver continued shouting back to the policemen. The loud and vocal dialogue between our driver and the policemen continued longer than we desired.

We were seated in the back of the car, listening and observing the present threatening dilemma. I took Gordon's hand, and we signaled to each other not to say a word but pray and stay in faith for our deliverance. One young policeman opened the car door next to me, and it appeared he was going to drag me out. But it was as if no one could touch us. We were under the Blood of Jesus.

We didn't give way to panic; the Lord surrounded us with great peace and we sensed we were enveloped in a bubble of divine protection. During all the shouts and threats, a yellow luxury car suddenly appeared to the left of us, stopped, and a man dressed in West African attire stepped out. With gestures of one in authority, he pointed his finger in the direction of the policemen. His demeanor was bold, his words rang out loud and clear, and we sensed he spoke in the dialect of the policemen. Suddenly, the policemen fled in terror and the unknown man drove off as quickly as he appeared. Our driver stepped on the accelerator, and we sped down the road to the hotel. Our driver told us he did not know who the man was, he had never seen him before.

We believe with great conviction that the man who appeared on that dark night was an angel sent by the Lord to deliver us. We praised God for rescuing us out of a terrifying nightmare. Angels are real, and they often appear as ordinary human beings. They minister and deliver those who are heirs of salvation. It has been known that believers have entertained angels unaware (Hebrews 13:2). The Word also says:

> Are they not all ministering spirits, sent forth to minister for them who shall be heirs of salvation? (Hebrews 1:14 KJV)

> For He shall give his angels charge over thee, to keep thee in all thy ways. (Psalm 91:11)

This experience on the mission field made the ministry of angels especially real to us.

A Visit to the Jungle

When the meetings in Port Harcourt concluded, we were told we were going down to the country for further meetings. It turned out to be down to the jungle on the Niger Delta to islands in the Kalabar region of Rivers State where the British were involved in the slave trade to America in the nineteenth century. The boat we travelled on was small and crowded, each person transporting goods home they bought in the city. Life vests were not to be seen. We quickly learned that safety precautions are few and far between. We passed miles of tropical rainforests populated by mangroves on each side of the river. Numerous fishermen were actively fishing the waters in their dugout boats, hauling in their daily catch. Others were taking care of their daily business rowing up and down the river beneath a cloudy sky and light rain showers.

When we first docked on the small island of Bakana, we were happily greeted by the church people, and escorted by foot to meet with the Christian tribal chief in his home. We were introduced to his family and attendants and greeted them according to their tribal protocol. Then we were asked to pray for him and his family. Afterward, we were led to the little local church for a meeting, preceded by a lunch of small fish pies prepared for us by the ladies. We learned to exercise strong faith when we prayed over our food, not always knowing what we were eating.

It was soon time to leave these precious people of God. We knew His Word had encouraged and built them up to receive and expect His promises to come to pass in their lives.

Walking through the village I noticed an extremely large black caldron, the kind you might see in cartoons of missionaries being boiled by the natives. I was tempted to stand behind the caldron facetiously, and have a photo taken, but we did not want to offend our brothers and sisters in the Lord. Vivid memories remain of our visit to this remote island.

Next, we boarded another boat to proceed to our next port of call. As we sped along the river, suddenly we saw a low bridge ahead of us adjoining two smaller islands. No one warned us of impending danger, but we quickly reacted by lowering our heads just in time to pass under the bridge. Otherwise we would have been decapitated and known as the "headless missionaries." Almost unbelievable!

The next island called Abonnema was larger with several little markets and stores on the main street. The locals were milling the streets, going about their daily tasks. We walked to a home where we stayed for the next few days. Many children greeted us quite surprised by seeing white folks for the first time. It was extremely hot and humid in this tropical jungle river area because of its close proximity to the equator.

Our bath was washing out of a small plastic bowl; there was a flush toilet but not a seat, quite common in the homes. We woke early each morning, aware that mosquitoes had visited us in the night, evidenced by small drops of blood on the sheets. The Lord kept us from contracting malaria or any tropical disease. We kept His Word on our lips and our faith in what the Blood of Jesus had done for us personally. The precious people of God always gave us the best food they had and lovingly cared for us, for which we were so thankful.

The church's electrical source was a generator as the electricity on the island did not function while we were there. We carried flash lights at night, enabling us to safely walk the village streets to and from the meetings. Often dogs would roam the streets, and we were reminded of what the nurse in London advised us before we came – to get a vaccination for rabies when we received other necessary vaccinations. We hadn't complied with her suggestion, but thankfully no dog ever came near us.

The church was filled each night. Time is not a factor in Africa. People will come late and stay for hours to hear the Word of God, sitting on hard, backless benches. Even the little children sat for hours, never falling off when sleep overtook them. We counted at least one hundred people received Jesus, and others were healed during these meetings.

We left the island of Abonnema rejoicing in all the Lord had done for these precious people. We boarded a boat to return to Port Harcourt. Someone mentioned that the captain had to be extraordinarily cautious at one part of the river as there are large rocks submerged when the tide is in, and boats were known to have crashed and all lives were lost. We were kept alert in praying without ceasing for our safety.

Several meetings were scheduled on our return to Port Harcourt. This time, we were guests in the home of a Shell Oil businessman and his wife. His large house was securely guarded by high walls with a security guard on duty day and night. Inside the house at the top of the stairs on the second floor was an iron gate like you would see in a prison. At night this was locked. We did wonder how we would escape if there was a fire or other emergency. One night I was awakened by the sound of something rustling in the room. I grabbed the flashlight and sure enough the culprit was a rat enjoying our snack food – he fled in fear of his life. That was the end of our munchies!

We were invited to dinner one evening as guests of a tribal chief and his family. We were extremely careful about the water we drank, making sure it was bottled. This particular night we were fooled because the bottles of water on the table were filled with tap water. Only after a few sips did we realize we were drinking local water. Oops! I had an opportunity to claim healing from an upset tummy that night. The meal was typical African, consisting of cassava root, escargot, fish, local greens, red beans, and periwinkle snails (from little cork screw shaped shells). We learned later that the seafood was probably contaminated with parasites. How conscious we were of God's protection over our food when we prayed!

Another special dinner on the agenda was held with church leaders and political dignitaries. This time we were presented with colorful Western African attire for the occasion. We adapted to the local protocol just as it was time to leave.

We flew back to Lagos for another meeting in one of the larger churches in the city. Our journey literally began racing down the road at a high speed in order to get to the airport on time for our flight. By the time we boarded the plane, the heavens opened and we got soaked in the deluge of rain while walking across the tarmac. Our host in Lagos took us to a hotel where we quickly changed and were whisked off to a large Lagos church. One more day of meetings and it was time to fly home to Putney. Mission accomplished, praise God!

Chapter 15

Our First Ministry in Europe

How glorious to see how the Lord positioned us in His plan and purpose. During our ministry visit to England in October and November 1988, we met an evangelist and his wife, Shiloh and Tita Haig, and their three small children from Australia. They were living in a few rooms in the damp basement of the church where we ministered on a Sunday night in South London. Shiloh asked us to pray for him, and the prophetic word came forth with great comfort for this family of God. They had desperate needs, including a home. We left them and believed God to watch over His Word to perform it in their lives. At that time, Shiloh's ministry was mainly in Europe and Asia.

One day in early 1991, Gordon quite unexpectedly had a phone call from Shiloh. He heard we were living in London, and the Lord told him to phone us. Gordon wondered what was on his mind. He told us that the prophetic word we spoke over him in November 1988 had come to pass. The Lord had opened the door for them to rent a nice home down on the Kent coast. He was rejoicing in the Lord for all He had provided for him and his family.

The next thing Shiloh shared was quite amazing – he wanted to help us minister in Europe and said he was recommending the churches where he ministered to have us minister there, too. How excited we were. It was an open door we knew we should go through. On March 9, 1991 we were on our way to Western Europe for the first time. The exciting journey that lay ahead of us began with a coach ride from London to the Hovercraft in Dover, Kent. It was a fast smooth crossing that day, and after forty five minutes we landed in Calais, France. Here we boarded another coach for our first destination: Antwerp, Belgium.

We were met by Pastor Andrew Chang who warmly welcomed us to the Chinese church. The family lived on the third and fourth floors of the church building. What fun we had carrying our luggage up all flights of stairs. At breakfast the following day, Pastor Andrew's young son was quite intrigued by Gordon's hairy arms, loudly shouting to his dad, "Hey Dad, he's got mustache all over his arms!"

The Sunday morning service was brief due to the church members owning and employing workers in the restaurant business. It was a challenge to be interpreted, first into Mandarin followed by Cantonese. Our daily menu was delicious Chinese food. In the afternoon, we were driven to

Brussels to minister at another Chinese church with Pastor Timothy Tang. The mid-week meeting in Antwerp started at midnight; the people could not attend until after closing down their restaurants. In spite of the lateness of the hour, the people eagerly listened to the Word and received the ministry of the Holy Spirit with joy. Each meeting was accompanied by salvations and prophetic ministry.

The time came to leave Belgium, and onward we proceeded to board a fast, comfortable train to Paris. After arriving at Garde du Nord station, we got a taxi to a suburb, Saint Denis. The rush hour traffic was horrendous. Our next accommodation was booked for us at the modest Formula One Motel. The next day Pastor Michael Molenda and his parents warmly welcomed us with a driving tour around Paris, where we had a chance brief encounter with French President Metieron on the corner of one of the streets.

We were ready and excited to be in this unreached part of the world with hope and faith in our hearts for God to manifest His love and mercy to a people who have been sitting in darkness for so many centuries. Our meetings at the church in La Blanc Mesnil, a mission church where they reach out to people from Romania, Guadeloupe, Martinique, and the gypsies. We experienced a first; people baptized in water in a bath tub at the back of the church. Three university students, one Algerian and two Vietnamese, attended the service for the purpose of researching Pentecostalism for their sociology class. We believe the Word they heard that morning, and the answers to their questions will not return void.

The ministry went well, and we again ministered through an interpreter. It was evident that they were not too happy with a woman ministering, so I only sang and joined with Gordon in interpreting the prophetic utterances in tongues. Five people were saved in the Saturday evening service, and three were saved on Sunday morning.

After the weekend meetings we were on our way to Grenoble, an eight hour road trip with the Molenda's in their van. The scenery along the French countryside was picturesque. Spring was about to burst on the land. In the southwest of France, the striking French Alps were still topped with winter's snow. We had a magnificent view of Mont Blanc, the highest mountain in Western Europe. Grenoble was the home of the 1968 Olympics.

We were there for a minister's convention attended by seven hundred ministers from several Francophone nations. A Grenoble church hosted the conference in the mountain town of San Laurent du Pont. The atmosphere was permeated with religious tradition, but we were ready to obey the Lord. Gordon ministered in one of the afternoon meetings. When he finished, he called me up to the platform to minister alongside him in the prophetic through tongues and interpretation. I already knew in my spirit what was about to happen, and I was ready to be used by the Lord. I covered my head with a scarf, as all women are taught to do in this particular denomination. It is important they do not take offense but receive the Word of God. The "head covering" teaching for women is still strong in some churches in Europe. This is another religious bondage women suffer based on lack of knowledge.

After a prophetic word went forth in the gifts of the Holy Spirit, Gordon invited any ministers who would like to hear from the Lord to come forward and be ministered to. A few brave, hungry pastors gingerly stepped up, and we proceeded to minister to them and left the results with the Holy Spirit. We were not there to please men but God. In such a large conference as this, the women are seen but definitely not heard.

The pastors were not exactly in favor of women preachers. In fact, they were quite hostile in their religious way. It did not deter us at all; we were established and confident in our calling and ministry as a husband-and-wife team. The Lord had already spoken to our spirits that His Word would always prevail despite any culture, tradition, or religious persuasions. Nothing could successfully stand against the Truth. We have always sought to obey the Lord, even in the midst of religious bondage and tradition. In 2 Corinthians 13:8 (AMP) says, *"For we can do nothing against the Truth [not serve any party or personal interest], but only for the Truth [which is the Gospel]."*

On Easter Sunday, we were driven to a church in a town snuggled high in the snow covered French Alps where the people were enthused about celebrating the resurrection of our Lord Jesus Christ. Following the service, the congregation enjoyed the traditional Easter lamb dinner followed by an afternoon meeting.

On the previous evening Gordon received a telephone call from the pastor of the church, asking him various questions regarding me. He had heard that I was also a minister and sometimes spoke in church, and he was greatly disturbed that I might say something in his church. The pastor's concern was that if I said anything, half of his church would walk out of the meeting. We thought we knew how strong this anti-women teaching prevailed in the country, but never for once did we think it was quite this radical. So Gordon wisely told the pastor that I would be coming with him but would not be preaching.

How can you silence the ministry of the Holy Spirit? Here were a group of believers who were in desperate need to hear from the Lord, and He had sent them a husband-and-wife team who could teach, preach, and minister together in the prophetic anointing. What were we to do? On one hand, we did not want to disrespect the pastor's authority, but on the other hand quench the Holy Spirit. Gordon ministered under a strong anointing in the morning service, and I remained silent but prayed quietly in tongues most of the time. Oh, how thankful we were to be able to draw on the wisdom of God.

After the Easter meal, we met for the afternoon service. Gordon asked permission for me to sing in the service, which was gracefully allowed. As I sang in English, I asked the translator to translate the meaning of the song into French, so all could understand. I took time, line upon line, to explain the meaning, inserting exhortation along the way. No one could argue against the song being translated into their language. How wise is our Heavenly Father in leading me to do this. Then Gordon proceeded to minister the Word.

We knew the Holy Spirit was grieved that day, and sadly, we could not minister as a team to the people in the prophetic gifts because of error of Bible doctrine concerning the ministry of women in the church. The ignorance of the knowledge of the Word of God had robbed the people of the comfort, edification, and exhortation ministry of the Gifts of the Holy Spirit (1 Corinthians 14:2-4). The ministry of the Spirit is so precious and holy, and not to be grieved. One cannot criticize the true supernatural utterances of the Spirit without repercussions. Sad to say, we learned later some pastors and church leaders were criticizing our ministry that day. We continued to walk in love and prayed for these precious people of God.

What we observed when we looked at the women was sadness and a sense of being unfulfilled. Fear filled their eyes, but at the same time there was a longing to be used of God and stepping over into the liberty of the sons and daughters of God. When women are not taught correctly from the Scriptures, they will remain immature, stunted in their spiritual development, and unable to fulfill their God-given calling.

Several years later, we were ministering in a church in Paris where the pastors are a wonderfully anointed husband-and-wife team. Many lined up at the close of the service to be ministered to for healing and the prophetic word. As we were about to minister to a man, he stopped and told us what had happened to him. He was one of the ministers who criticized us that day at the pastors' convention in Grenoble. He had repented but had suffered greatly in the loss of family and ministry and was at that time quite sick. He asked us to forgive him. Of course, we did and then proceeded to minister to him, believing the Lord would restore him in every way.

After the ministers' convention in Grenoble, our road trip continued east on the Monday morning with Roger and Jackie Danois to the east coast of France. Jackie was the pastor of a church in Bayonne. The long journey included magnificent scenery, ancient castles, and a view of the Pyrenees Mountains. During two days of ministry in the church we were treated royally with gourmet French food.

Gordon's heartfelt desire was to minister in the small villages and towns that were out of the way places where well known evangelists did not go, and he was now living out this God given desire. His heart was filled with the love of God to minister to the ones and twos as well as the large crowds.

It was time to go to Spain for a Sunday evening service. The cold rain pelted the windscreen as we crossed into the Basque region of northern Spain. Many in the congregation were Para-military people in this politically sensitive region. The Finish pastor welcomed the ministry of the Word, and we laid hands on the people for healing. The pastor's wife received her healing that night. An invitation was extended to return for three days' ministry in October of that year.

There were other churches in the Grenoble area who had scheduled us to return. This time during another long train journey across the south of France, we were delayed in changing trains at Narbonne as the train from Spain was late. Our first meeting was thirty miles away from Grenoble, so we quickly readied ourselves to go to La Cate de St André, a medieval town with narrow streets. The church, although new, received the Word. One young lady was delivered of demons. A knee was healed, and the swelling went down immediately. Another was baptized in the Holy Spirit. In Voreppe the following evening, two young men were saved and others were ministered to in the prophetic.

The following afternoon we traveled fifty miles through two mountain passes that allowed us breathtaking views as the sun was going down. We arrived at the mountain town of Die, an old Roman town of 5,000 people. The church was small but our wonderful Lord brought living water to the thirsty.

The next day we were guests on Radio Certitude, owned by the Grenoble church. I sang and we shared the Word together with freedom in the Spirit. Our translator, Francois, and his wife Veronica, gave us a tour around the Chartreuse Mountains.

The mountain meadows were blooming with primroses and crocus; there was still sufficient snow on the higher elevations for the last of the winter skiers.

A church in Strasbourg was awaiting our visit, and it was time to board the train and head north to our next assignment. After blessed meetings in this historic city on the German border, we prepared for another long train ride to the English Channel. Changing trains in Lyon proved difficult. There was no elevator, so we had to carry our luggage up the stairs, cross the bridge, and head down another flight of stairs. Gordon accidentally let go of my suitcase and it bounced down each step crashing at the bottom. Thankfully, there was nothing missing and nothing broken. Finally arriving in Calais, we boarded the ferry to Dover; onward to London on another train. We were filled with joy and praise for God's protection and blessings. We were homeward bound as the taxi from Victoria station maneuvered through the busy streets of London to Putney.

What ensued as a result of our first ministry to Belgium, France, and Spain were many open doors extending into Switzerland and Denmark. A few years later we ministered in Lanzarote, one of the Canary Islands, and the island of Cyprus. Each country has its own language, culture, and traditions— even food. It is an adventure in itself. We were now getting used to flying back and forth into Europe and using the fast TGV trains across France.

Chapter 16
Ministry in Pakistan and Kenya

God is so faithful! Despite many obstacles, in November 1990, we were finally on our way to Pakistan via Mumbai, India, previously called Bombay. We persevered through a flight delay at London's Heathrow airport. Finally the Air India plane taxied down the runway but suddenly turned back for engine repairs. We are filled with excitement and thanksgiving to our Heavenly Father, knowing we are in His care and protection. This necessitated staying at a hotel overnight near the airport; the flight finally left the following morning.

When you leave a day late it puts your schedule off. We could not meet our ongoing scheduled flights to Karachi and Faisalabad. It also meant we did not have a visa to leave Mumbai airport in order to spend another night at a hotel. At midnight, we maneuvered through two hours of red tape, trusting the favor of the Lord, to obtain a temporary visa, leaving our passports with the customs authorities. We were now free to leave the airport and sleep at a nearby hotel provided by Air India.

The bumpy bus ride at 2 a.m. was a culture shock as we pass so many people sleeping on the streets in squalor. We were very thankful for four hours of sleep followed by breakfast. Another bumpy ride and we were back at the airport. The bright sunlight revealed numerous people occupied with daily life, cars dodging rickshaws, motor bikes, and cows. Small Hindu temples are frequently positioned along the streets. We were not used to the obnoxious odors.

At last we were on our way to Pakistan after recovering our passports. It was an uneventful short flight of one and half hours to Karachi. We requested our onward flight to Faisalabad that day, and praise God, He provided two seats. We were met by the pastor's wife and a doctor from the church. In their small van, we continued our journey to the Rex Hotel, located in the center of the city, our home for one night. The streets were chaotic and dangerous as we passed cows, oxen, horses, and camels drawing wagons of hay, wood, textiles, and other local commodities. We were determined to get used to the noise coming from the streets as the people celebrated the inauguration of a new prime minister. At five o'clock in the morning we were awakened by the sounds of loud prayers coming from the local mosque.

A crusade had been arranged in a town four hours away. The journey on a rough, bumpy road kept us alert and praying.

We encountered a few near misses as our driver maneuvered down the dusty road, passing brightly decorated buses, trucks called lorries, bicycles, and scooters. Passengers cling to the crowded buses, some riding on the roof, as they also do on the trains. We zoom past camel trains laden with local goods. Children delight in running after the lorries, grabbing stalks of sugar cane from the overflowing loads. The flat topography of the land appears agriculturally fruitful. Fields abounded with sugar cane, cotton, corn, rice, orange groves, and rapeseed. The crops are irrigated with the assistance of the camels. Women mainly work the fields, harvesting the rice and other crops. The people are milling everywhere, and the air is filled with swarms of flies. We took note of the brick factories and sugar cane mills along the way.

The homes, either square or rectangular, are built in Middle Eastern style; some constructed from mud, others brick. Cow dung is formed by hand into patties by the women and children, and then placed on the walls and outside of homes to dry to be used for fuel, which included cooking their food.

Our first stop is at the home of Pastor Daniel in Sargodah. Christians live in communities, known as "Christian colonies," situated in the poorest section of town. Many sweet children greet us as we walked down the dusty neighborhood streets. A tasty lunch is awaiting us—fried rice, curried potatoes, and chapatti bread, accompanied by cups of hot tea.

We arrive in Mandi Bahauddin around five in the afternoon and are taken to a guest house at Shahtag Sugar Mill located a little distance outside of town in a secure area. It is clean and comfortable with a ceiling fan to help keep us cool. The grounds of the sugar mill remind us of a British colonial estate, beautifully manicured with an abundance of bougainvilleas and other exotic flowers. I notice I am the only woman on the grounds. The Muslim waiter treated us with favor, took care of our needs, and brought meals to our room.

The crusade meetings are held in the street, enclosed with colorful tent coverings. Rugs cover the street with men sitting on one side and women on the other, and everyone's shoes are left in the aisle. I am asked to give a brief greeting, my head covered with a light chiffon scarf and shoes removed, followed by my preaching to a crowd of about four hundred. We prayed for many sick folks, and Gordon and the doctor laid hands on the men. One of the ladies and I laid hands on the women.

An outstanding deliverance from demon possession took place that night. A beautiful young Muslim woman writhed on the floor like a snake. Gordon told the people not to be afraid and believe God's Word. When we laid hands on this young woman, her body continued to coil then stopped, with her head resting by Gordon's shoe. We took authority over the demons holding her in bondage. When Gordon touched her she felt cold and lifeless. In faith, we praised God that she was delivered and we proceeded to return to rest at our lodging for the night. The next night, the people excitedly came up to us, reporting that a little after we left, she came out of the trance, totally free, and asked Jesus into her heart. When we met her, her face was shining with the presence of the Lord. She testified how the Lord had delivered her from demon power.

The next day we ministered in the afternoon and evening services. Two hundred responded for salvation, followed by praying for the sick in mass. We were so thrilled to see the Muslim people respond to the Gospel and receive Jesus. We thanked the Lord for such a fruitful day.

We were taken to another community the next morning to minister to a Christian family whose twelve year old son had died. The Muslim men from the community had gathered at the house in sympathy. It gave an opportunity for Gordon to present the Gospel to them and pray for healing for one of the men who asked for prayer.

The next stop was a government hydro housing community to hold a service in a church. Around one hundred crowded the small building, and we rejoiced as twenty responded for salvation. Our location was close to the Afghanistan border, and we had an excellent view of the distant mountains. The river, which provided the hydro dam, looked more like a sewage disposal. Men fished here, women washed their clothes, and cows cooled themselves, all in the same water. Vultures feasted on an oxen carcass. The local food market displayed beef carcasses covered in flies.

I preached in the afternoon open air crusade meeting on Mark 5:25-34, how hearing the Word builds faith to receive healing, like the woman with the issue of blood. Many stood to receive their healing; others received Jesus into their hearts.

Gordon preached in the evening meeting and ministered to a large crowd, around 1,000 attendants. Three hundred stood for salvation. When the meeting concluded, we were asked to go from house to house to pray over the Christians' homes. Donkeys brayed a welcome sound as we navigated by foot through the narrow lanes. We laid hands on many with debilitating diseases, such as tuberculosis, typhoid, and yellow fever. We were refreshed with a cup of tea and cookies in one of the homes, with loving hospitality.

God wonderfully provided for us at the guest house. A Christian worker at the sugar mill asked favor for us with the owners, and they did not charge us for our stay. The Muslim people provided for us to preach the Gospel in their land!

It was time to return to Faisalabad. On our way we stopped at Sargodah to visit Pastor Daniel again and received warm hospitality and lunch. We could not get away until I was fitted for a Punjabi outfit, handmade by one of the ladies. Her sewing spot was on a bed in the courtyard where she creatively sewed her garments.

We are now back at the Rex Hotel where we settle in for a much needed rest and preparation for the next meetings. Sundays are busy shopping days at the bazaars in the downtown area of the city. It was fun to shop for gifts. We were graciously treated to dinner at the pastor's home, this time delicious Chinese food.

The Faisalabad meetings were strongly anointed. The people always responded to the invitation for salvation and prayer for healing. Though tired, we would meet with the ministers and their families after the meetings in the hotel restaurant for a meal together. It was always a good time of fellowship, sharing, and laughing together. We may come from different cultures and speak different languages, but there was a strong, loving bond in the family of God.

On November 14, it was time to leave for the airport for our flight back to Karachi. On the way, we stopped to pray over the land the ministry purchased for their headquarters and church building. The prophetic word came forth for the staff concerning what the Lord was going to do for them. The brothers and sisters were greatly encouraged. In due time, all came to pass, and today they have their ministry center and church building.

Karachi is a large city, situated on the Arabian Sea. The architecture is influenced by British colonialism. We are met by one of the pastors. They hired a van to transport us around. We could have stayed in a hotel but chose to stay in one of the pastor's homes for the night. They lovingly welcomed us into their small home, consisting of an enclosed courtyard, two rooms, a small kitchen, and a room with a toilet and a washing area next to it. A ladder in the courtyard gave access to the roof with three rooms where another family lived. Seventeen people lived in this home, and we made nineteen that night. They gave us the best room with two single beds and their finest linen.

After tea and a snack we were off to a meeting in a village on the outskirts of Karachi. Fifteen of us packed into the small Suzuki van, travelling over very rough roads. We disembark and proceed to walk down a dark, narrow lane, avoiding cow patties and who knows what else. God's love and abundant grace is more than enough to meet our present circumstances. The service was held in the courtyard of one of the homes with dim lights and dirty mats. People began coming and coming, until around 250 gathered to hear the Word. That night seventy people responded to the salvation invitation. We laid hands on many and ministered to them in the prophetic.

We arrived back at the pastor's home where they graciously prepared a supper of rice, curried chicken, and potatoes. We knew we were partaking of their best. The pastor said they could not afford rice and meat every day. Their diet usually consists of chapattis and vegetables.

Our sleep is not exactly sound that night. We are aware that rats likely lived somewhere in the walls—thankfully they were not to be seen. We were awakened by the sound of early morning Muslim prayers. Our breakfast of boiled eggs is welcomed with more chapatti bread and tea. The driver of the van arrives to take us on a tour of Karachi and a visit to the beach on the Arabian Sea. We passed up the opportunity of riding a camel. It was extremely hot that day, and I remember walking with one of the young daughters of the pastor. As I held her hand, I was so aware of the sweet love of Jesus for these precious people and their love for us.

It is time to say goodbye to our precious brothers and sisters. Joy filled our hearts as we thanked them for their loving care for us. We made so many friendships and memories. Most of all, we were so thankful for all the Lord did: the salvations—fourteen hundred were saved, many healings, and encouraging prophetic words to lift and comfort the people of God in Pakistan.

Good News Women's Seminar in Faisalabad, Pakistan (November 12 and 13, 1990)

It is a hot dry afternoon in Faisalabad. The air was filled with dust, and flies are swarming everywhere. There is an excitement in my spirit as our driver skillfully maneuvers through the bustling, noisy streets of the city. Dodging donkey carts, camels, and horses seems no challenge to our driver. Then there are the many cars, brightly decorated buses, and lorries to cope with. We were nearing our destination. "How much further?", I thought, as we leave the pothole-filled dirt streets to make our way past homes where there are no proper roads. Their owners are milking large, black cows, and many small children outside their meager homes are happily entertaining chickens and goats.

The car finally stopped beside a pair of donkeys, and it is time to disembark and make our way towards the little brick church on the next corner. Many women were gathering for the Good News Women's Seminar held in a roofless church. Brightly colored mats are laid over the uneven brick floor so the women can sit more comfortably. There were no chairs to be found except a few for their western guests. Sitting on the floor is not an unusual custom in this land. Shoes are left in the small aisle, according to tradition. I remove my shoes before stepping on to the platform to minister.

I thought, "Where in the world am I"? My heart is filled with such joy and excitement as I realized the time has come to teach the Word of God to a beautiful group of women. This is the first day of a two day seminar. The women sit with expectation to hear the good news. Here I was in a country I had envisioned as a child. I had long ago known that I would someday minister in this land. This country was part of India when I was young. God's Word to me is being fulfilled before my eyes.

I am in one of the major cities in Pakistan. My head was covered with a white chiffon scarf in the tradition of the eastern culture. As I walked down the aisle toward the podium, red rose petals were thrown over me. Young beautiful schoolgirls, dressed in sparkling national costumes, sang welcome songs with hands outstretched, showing their love to their western visitor. A garland of red roses is placed around my neck. How God's love flowed from my heart to theirs.

It was time to teach and minister the Word of Life to many hungry women. I know they have been prepared by the Holy Spirit to receive that day. As the Word was conveyed through my translator, I sensed the Holy Spirit was convincing those who needed to be born again to receive Jesus. Yes, praise God, twenty women boldly stood to their feet and openly asked Jesus into their hearts. The rest of the lovely women, who already knew the Lord, were edified and encouraged as they learned who they are as women of God in Christ; not someone unworthy with little value but God's workmanship, a new creation, and someone special in the eyes of the Lord. I laid hands on many to receive healing in their bodies. So many were sick and needed miracles that day; I point them to Jesus, the Healer, who meets their needs and confirms His Word.

Darkness was quickly descending as the meeting came to a close, and the women were now making their way home—some walking, others travelling in small carts pulled along by their donkeys. As the sun set, I noticed bats swooping down on our gathering. It reminded me of the enemy who comes immediately to steal the Word out of the hearts of God's people (Mark 4:15). With a quick prayer, I bound the enemy and commanded the spiritual birds of prey to be gone and on their way.

The following day many more women gathered, about 150. They satt attentively as I taught them how they can pray in faith in the Name of Jesus and receive answers to prayer for themselves. They learned how to release their faith through speaking His Word and acting on the Word of God to receive the desired results. Hearing the simplicity of the Gospel caused faith to come into their hearts, and they returned home with a fresh hope and confidence in the goodness of our Father God. What a privilege it was to have had a lasting impact in the lives of the beautiful women in Pakistan.

Kenya, East Africa (November 1990)

We arrived at the Karachi airport early. It gave us time to unwind, refresh, and relax before our flight to Nairobi, Kenya. The airport restaurant offers a few western items; the cheese sandwich tasted so good.

When we shared our adventures with a doctor friend in California he said, "You shouldn't have eaten the cheese."

When we asked him why he said, "You could have contracted tuberculosis!"

We ate in faith, and the Lord protected us. When we mentioned how thankful we were to have a shower in the hotel in Faisalabad, the doctor was quick to tell us, "You shouldn't have showered with the water because you could have picked up parasites, and they could have worked their way into your liver."

We are so thankful we had inside information—faith in the Blood of Jesus and the Word of God. He truly preserved us.

It is time to board our flight. We were excited to be on our way to visit John and Elizabeth and their sons, David and Erik. A short stop-over in Abu Dhabi allowed us to dismount for twenty minutes and walk around the luxurious, gold embellished duty free area. We finally arrived in Nairobi at 11:30 at night local time to cool, rainy weather in the high elevation of the city. We were met by our excited family. It took an hour and a half to collect our luggage, making for a late night.

The missionaries' colonial home on the campus of Pan African Christian College is a welcome sight. A shower and clean bed under mosquito netting provides a wonderful sleep. We looked forward to Elizabeth's home cooking.

The next morning, we were up early and prepared for the chapel service on campus. I ministered in song and Gordon brought a brief message to the students. The rest of the day is spent acclimating with a walk and rest.

On Saturday, November 17, we thoroughly enjoyed a visit to Lake Naivasha, traveling on fairly good roads. Kenya enjoys a varied topography – mountains and plains filled with colorful flowering trees and bushes, not to forget the beautiful tropical coastline on the Indian Ocean. We passed lush verdant coffee and tea plantations before stopping for a picnic near the lake where zebras were spotted.

We drove on to Elsamere, the former home of Joy Adamson, an author and naturalist. It was a beautiful area populated with Colobus monkeys jumping through the euphorbia trees. Tropical birds we had never seen before are in abundance. Papyrus grasses grow in profusion around the lakeside. Elizabeth and John pointed out that hippopotamuses are frequent visitors, but they chose not to make an appearance while we were there. It was a much needed, relaxing, and delightful day of family fun.

Pastor Dennis White of the Nairobi Pentecostal Church welcomed us in the Sunday morning service, followed by ministry at the Sunday evening service. The Sunday morning services average 6,000 attendees with a good number attending in the evening. Gordon ministered on Bible prosperity, spirit, soul, body, and financial blessings (3 John 2). We prayed for the sick in mass as well as believing for the financial needs of the people to be met.

We toured Nairobi's downtown. It is filled with vestiges of British colonial days as well as modernization in some areas, not forgetting the large slum area where many live. Our visit would not be complete without a visit to the Nairobi Game

Park with John and Elizabeth as our tour guides. The abundance of indigenous animals and birds in the wild are amazing to behold. We did not see any lions but are sure they were somewhere grazing on the vast grasslands. We are warned to be aware of snakes. A big black mamba was found and killed in the college chapel while we were visiting. The high altitude and fresh air caused us to tire easily, and it is not difficult to sleep.

It was time to return to London on November 24. Our eight and a half hour flight took us over the Sudan, Egypt, Turkey, Crete, Thessalonica, Yugoslavia, Switzerland, and Austria. The Alps were covered in snow; it was back to winter in Britain with high temperatures around forty-two degrees.

Chapter 17

The Islands of the Sea

Let them give glory unto the Lord, and declare his praise in the islands.   *−Isaiah 42:1*

Bermuda

The Lord has a unique way of surprising His children. We never once thought about going to the beautiful island of Bermuda to minister or to enjoy a vacation. We had no friends or acquaintances living on this spectacular sub-tropical paradise.

On our return to London from ministering in Nigeria in 1990, we were invited to minister at a Nigerian church in East London. At the close of the service, a young man introduced himself, identifying his country of origin as Bermuda. He had been blessed by our ministry and desired to have fellowship with us as he was working in London for a season. We were pleased to get to know Melvin Alick. It turned out to be a relationship that led to many doors opening for ministry in Bermuda and making special friendships there with the people of God.

Bermuda is the first of the countries colonized by the British after being discovered by the Spanish explorer Juan de Bermúdez in 1503, the first known European to discover this archipelago. Although usually referred to in the singular, the territory consists of 181 islands, the islands being named after Bermdúez. He claimed the apparently uninhabited islands for the Spanish Empire. Although he paid two visits, Bermúdez never landed on the islands, because he did not want to risk crossing over the dangerous reef surrounding them. It was founded by the British in the aftermath of a hurricane in July 1612, when Admiral George Somers and the crew of the sinking *Sea Venture,* a seventeenth-century English sailing ship on its way to Jamestown, Virginia, steered the ship onto the reef, so they could get ashore.

The islands became a British colony in 1707. After 1949, when Newfoundland became part of Canada, Bermuda automatically was ranked as the oldest remaining British overseas territory. Today it is the most populous territory. Its first capital, St. George's, was established in 1612 by the Virginia Company and is the oldest continuously inhabited English town in the New World. St. Peter's Church, in St. George's, is the oldest surviving Anglican Church in continuous use outside the British Isles. It is also reportedly the oldest continuously used Protestant church in the New World (Wikipedia).

Our first of many ministry visits to Bermuda began in August 1991. As we flew in from New York, a panoramic view revealed the many tropical-colored homes – pink, turquoise, yellow, green, and blue – scattered throughout the islands. The brilliant white roofs are used as catchments for rain water, draining into each home's underground cistern. This is their primary source of water.

Every time we visited, a precious couple, Gerald and Ruth Paynter, welcomed us to stay at their colonial-style accommodation, Clear View Suites and Villas. Our view on the north shore gave us the advantage of stunning sunrises and magnificent sunsets overlooking the clear azure waters of the Atlantic Ocean. Several times a week the cruise ships sailed by, carefully guided into port by a tug boat through a narrow passage, thus avoiding the dangerous reefs, and then they safely dock into Hamilton's port. The beaches on the north and south shores are literally a landscape of pink sand by the warm waters of the Gulf Stream.

We ministered in several churches: the traditional African Methodist Episcopal and other churches, including Pentecostal denominations. Each time we preached and taught the Word, the people responded with a genuine hunger to learn and grow in the Lord. A camp meeting held in a tent at Shelly Bay was well attended. The Lord opened the door for us to be interviewed on local television, and further doors were wide open for us to minister. The majority of Bermudans are church goers, but we found that many did not understand the reality of the new birth. It was such a joy to see so many respond to the preaching of the Gospel and receive Jesus as Lord and Savior. We taught on the baptism in the Holy Spirit and how to receive their healing through faith in the Word of God and the Name of Jesus.

God Knows Our Address

But my God shall supply all your need according to his riches in glory by Christ Jesus.
– Philippians 4:19

I recall a time when Gordon and I had a pressing need. It was a personal need for $3,000, and it was not something for the ministry. We were ministering in Bermuda and told no one about our need. We had prayed and believed we received this money based on Mark 11:23-24.

We gratefully received the offering from a church where we ministered on Sunday, which greatly blessed our ministry, but it did not meet our personal need. Monday morning arrived and there was a knock at the door where we were staying. A gentleman who had heard us minister in church the previous day came to bring us good news. He was led of the Holy Spirit to give us a check for the exact amount we needed to meet our need. The Holy Spirit knew our need, He knew the exact place where we were staying, and sent a man to bless us. You can imagine the rejoicing that ensued on that day!

Father God knows where you live, and He knows how to get the money and provisions to you. Sometimes it can be through a stranger and through the most unusual circumstances.

Nearly every year we returned to Bermuda to minister in the local churches, meeting new pastors each time. On two occasions we put on our own meeting in the Conference Room at Clear View. It was here that I spoke to the Women's Aglow chapter.

In August of 1998 I hosted a Faith Women International conference at Clear View with speakers coming from various nations. We welcomed long time friend Pat Carver, whom I worked with in Women's Aglow during our years in Atlanta, Georgia. Other women speakers included Nancy Glass, whose friendship goes back to 1976 when we helped pioneer her and Paul's church in Rex, Georgia. Maria Rossi, our intercessory prayer coordinator and translator into French, flew in from Belgium. Ministers who worked with us in Guildford, England, including Mieke Colleé and Barb Witt joined us in supporting this teaching outreach to the island.

Lanzarote

Lanzarote is one of the Canary Islands, whose topography is volcanic with the Fire Mountains smoldering in spots. It is a popular destination for vacationers, especially the British. We had never thought of going there, but God had another plan. When we discerned the spiritual state of the island, we knew there needed to be a visitation of the fire of the Holy Spirit.

A couple from England, John and Evelyn Graham, were living in Lanzarote with a burning desire for the people of the island to hear the Gospel. Churches were small and needed encouragement. Through our dear friend and ministry associate, Mieke Colleé, we were invited to go and minister life-giving words. Our ministry associate, Barb Witt, joined us too.

We prayed and sought the Lord as to how to reach the people. We visited one or two of the little churches, but it seemed the Lord wanted us to hold meetings in the Graham's home. The invitation went out and we preached and taught the Word to those who came. Another meeting was an outreach to the women. It was hard ground to say the least. We prayed other laborers would come and water the Word.

Cyprus

In March of 2003 we had an invitation from Peter and Anne Graham in Portsmouth, England to join them for ministry on the island of Cyprus. It is the largest island in the Eastern Mediterranean Ocean, the third most populous island.

This Mediterranean island, a tourist attraction, is divided; the northern part is governed by Turkey and the southern area by

Greece. The island has an ancient history, first under the control of Egypt but later to be ruled by Rome. Greek mythology influenced the island with evidence of the cult of Aphrodite in Paphos.

Peter and Anne graciously hosted us during our stay and drove us to Mt. Olympus, the highest mountain on the island. It was cold and still covered in snow from the winter storms.

The most interesting history of Cyprus is found in the New Testament. The book of Acts tells us that the apostle Paul and Barnabas, who was a citizen of Cyprus, preached on the island on their missionary journey. (Acts 4:36; 11:19-20; 13:4; 15:39; 27:4.)

Did you know that Lazarus, whom Jesus loved and raised from the dead, went to Larnaca in Cyprus? He escaped death because the chief priests threatened to kill him when many of the Jews believed in Jesus as recorded in John 12:1-11. Lazarus was buried for a second time beneath a tiny church on the site of the present Ayios Lazaros church in Larnaca, his tomb was inscribed with, *Lazarus four days dead and friend of Christ.* (Wikipedia)

It was such a honor to minister on this historic island knowing who had gone before us as recorded in the book of Acts. The meetings in the church in Limassol were attended by hungry people, some of whom came from India and the Middle East. We faithfully sowed the incorruptible seed of the Word of God, the Lord confirming His Word with manifestations of the Holy Spirit.

Chapter 18

More Open Doors of Ministry in Europe

Much of our ministry in the 1990's was in the Western European countries. Many opportunities lay before us as one church would be a catalyst for us to go into many other churches. News spread of how the Holy Spirit was moving and bringing people into the glorious liberty of salvation, healing, and wholeness.

France

We regularly ministered in France, from Paris in the north to the southern cities, beginning at Bayonne near Biarritz on the Bay of Biscay and Bordeaux. Saint-Gaudens close to the Pyrenees mountains onward to Toulouse, and a number of towns surrounding Toulouse, such as, Albi, Auch, Agen, Castres and Cahor, were included in our ministry itinerary. We were also blessed to minister in Strasbourg and towns in

Our Love Journey

the Lorraine and Alsacs regions bordering the Rhine River and Germany. They proved fruitful in ministry. The Lorraine region is the home of Joan of Arc.

It was an adventure to travel on the fast TGV trains throughout France. Otherwise, we flew into a major town, and transportation was provided for us through the churches. The medieval cathedrals with exquisite artwork and majestic architecture caught our eye. Was there a move of God in days gone by, or were these cathedrals just relics to be admired? A brief history of these godly believers follows.

God raised up the Huguenots. They had their origin in sixteenth-century France. Huguenots were French Protestants who were inspired by the writings of John Calvin, and they endorsed the Reformed tradition of Protestantism. Huguenot numbers peaked near an estimated two million by 1562, concentrated mainly in the southern and western parts of France. The bulk of Huguenot emigrants relocated to Protestant states such as England, Wales, Scotland, Denmark, Sweden, Switzerland, the Dutch Republic, and other nations. (Wikipedia)

The churches and cathedrals seemed like sepulchers, filled with dead religious tradition. History tells us God raised up great reformers such as Martin Luther, John Hus, John Calvin, John Wycliffe, William Tyndale, and many others. What would they think of the present spiritual climate in Europe? We sensed it was time for God to move in revival power and reveal Himself as the Almighty God, Prince of Peace, and Coming King.

So many questions we pondered in our hearts on each visit to these cities and towns. There was definitely a need for the ground to be ploughed and broken up, followed by sowing the incorruptible seed of the Word, and watering it with further teaching to bring forth the much needed harvest.

We found the churches in Paris, pastored by French speaking Africans from Zaire, the Congo, and the French West Indies, were hungry and teachable. Their praise music was happy and free. Their hearts were open to hear from the Spirit of God.

We met Pastors Marc and Annemarie Lebrun in Paris in the early 90's. At that time they had recently planted a church in one of the Paris suburbs. Numerous times, we were hosted by this precious couple to minister to their small but growing church. There was always a freedom in the spirit to minister in teaching and in the gifts of the Holy Spirit. Each time we visited, the growth of the church was evident as the need for larger facilities continued. Their daughters, Elvira and Léa, were excellent in their translation when we ministered.

Belgium

In Belgium we were hosted several times by the Chinese churches, both in Antwerp and Brussels. Their love for the

Word of God was evidenced in each service. Mid-week services began at midnight and concluded at three in the morning. Why, you ask, would they meet at such a late hour? Most of the members owned restaurants and they were not available until midnight. Since part of the congregation spoke Mandarin and others Cantonese, it was necessary for our preaching to be translated from English to Mandarin, then into Cantonese, making for a short time to preach.

Pastors Andrew Chang and Pastors Timothy Tang were so gracious as they welcomed us into their midst. One summer, we were guest speakers for their annual camp meeting in Holland. There was a relaxed atmosphere in a fourteent- century castle where we stayed and ministered.

The Spirit of God moved in revival fire and power as the people fell down weeping and coming up with great joy as they shouted and rejoiced before the Lord. One man's leg, shorter than the other as a result of polio, was lengthened by God's miracle power. We ministered to many in the prophetic anointing, and several people were born again.

A Notable Miracle in Belgium

Mr. and Mrs. Chanh Giang of Enghein, Belgium, were no different from any other parents expecting the birth of their first child. They were filled with joy and hope as the day of their son's birth approached. Their dreams were shattered when Patrick was born.

He appeared to be a normal healthy boy at birth, but on the second day after his birth, the muscles in his body contracted, resulting in his brain not developing normally. The Doctor who observed him for twenty five days in the hospital said Patrick would have problems as a result, meaning he would be unable to walk, talk, and even suffer blindness, only distinguishing shadows of light and dark. He also was unable to hear in one ear. In fact, he was virtually paralyzed.

Where do parents turn in a situation like this? Does God still perform miracles today? Is there hope for their son?

It was March 10, 1991, and we spent some time explaining to the parents how to receive healing through the Word of God and how to stay in faith by confessing God's Word over their son until they saw the manifestation of his healing. We laid hands on Patrick according to Mark 16:18, "They shall lay hands on the sick, and they shall recover." We explained, according to this Scripture, he would recover.

Now, nothing visible happened. Patrick looked just the same—acted just the same—unable to walk, talk, hear and see. But that day, the parents caught hold of the revelation of how to stand in faith, and not be moved by what they saw or didn't see. They kept speaking the Word of God to their son. His father would often say to Patrick, "According to the Word of God you are healed. Now, you are going to walk."

His mother would say, "You are able to walk, your father is walking behind you, don't be afraid you can walk."

It was now May 9 and time for Patrick's check up at the hospital. But it was also time for a supernatural change in Patrick's body. On May 10, during Patrick's stay at the hospital, he suddenly jumped up out of the bed and started walking and running around the hospital. The doctor couldn't believe what he was seeing—God's miracle working power was affecting Patrick's body.

Today Patrick is walking and running. He has perfect eyesight, perfect hearing, and he is able to understand what is spoken to him and talk. In fact, he is speaking French more fluently than his native Chinese and attending school.

We visited Mr. and Mrs. Giang in July 1991 during ministry in that area and rejoiced together with them that their son was made whole by the power of God. Satan had come to steal, but Jesus had brought His miracle, life giving power to a little boy whose parents dared to believe God. At that time, they both expressed a desire to be baptized in the Holy Spirit according to the book of Acts. They both received and spoke in tongues.

You see, there are no hopeless situations, for Jesus is alive and the same yesterday, today, and forever. (Hebrews 13:8)

We had many invitations to minister in the French-speaking churches in Belgium. Each time the Holy Spirit ministered the Word into the lives of these precious people.

It was in a little church in La Bouverie in 1991 that we met a beautiful young lady whose heart was so hungry for the things of God. She skillfully interpreted for us in each service. We want to share her powerful testimony:

Maria Rossi Di Francesco

Little did I know when I first met Gordon and Barbara White in a little church in La Bouverie, Belgium in 1991, where I interpreted for them into French, that these two precious people were going to become an important part of my life.

I had no idea at that time that I would spend the following twelve years not only interpreting for them on their ministry trips to Belgium, but that I would also work for them. My ministry included translator into French, director of operations and intercession, and travelling with them in England, France, the United States, Holland, Belgium, Bermuda, and Israel. Besides that, I have had the privilege to minister alongside them.

We have spent countless hours sharing the Word of God, praying, dreaming, and rejoicing in the Lord. Our tea times at The Lodge in

Guildford, England, are some of my most precious memory gems

I know firsthand that what they preach and teach is what they live, because I saw them in their daily life. What a precious testimony to me! Their tenacity to the Word of God and their faithfulness to the Lord has been an example to me. The accuracy of the prophetic words they have ministered into the lives of thousands of people is amazing.

I know personally that the words that have come out of their mouths, through the gift of tongues and interpretation, are true words of the living God. I can testify that each prophetic utterance they released into my life has been fulfilled and sometimes in an unexpected way. Even today, in 2013, I have seen the fulfillment of prophetic words I received through them in 1992.

The Lord said to me, "For I have given you the hearing ear, says the Lord, but you shall not only hear the languages of nature, but you shall hear the languages of the Spirit and you shall have the interpretation from heaven."

Twenty-one years after the prophetic word was spoken over my life, God has suddenly opened the way for me to be involved in the prophetic intercession ministry in our church here in Italy. I have indeed started to hear the Spirit speak and give precise instructions on how to pray and what to do, through specific words of wisdom and words of knowledge. I give all the glory to God!

God will do what He has spoken through His prophets if we take heed, believe, proclaim, and hold on to His promises. We don't have to figure things out. God knows that some prophetic words I received years ago I did not understand. I, like Mary, pondered these things and kept them in my heart. I kept on believing that God's word would come to pass. Little did I know when I met Gordon and Barbara that they would become family to me.

I thank the Lord for sending them into my life! They have been my spiritual parents, loving me and encouraging me constantly. They have been my spiritual mentors, teaching me how to rightly divide the Word of truth. They have been my example of a life and ministry of integrity. Their love for God and for His Word has shaped my heart. I will be forever grateful to the Lord for precious people like Gordon and Barbara White.

With love and blessings,
Maria Rossi Di Francesco

Maria faithfully visited our ministry office in Guildford helping with the administrative work, translating our newsletter into French, and translating Gordon's book, *What On Earth are You saying?* into the French language.

Spain

While ministering in a church in Bayonne, France, we were asked by the pastor if we would like to minister in Spain. We joyfully accepted this opportunity. Since Bayonne is situated close to the Spanish border, it was a short journey into the Basque area of northern Spain. We were instructed not to use the name *Spain* due to the politically sensitive issues between Spanish and Basque people. We exercised wisdom while ministering and talking to the people.

Arrangements were made for us to return and minister in a number of Assembly of God churches in three cities. San

Sebastian is a popular resort town in the summer on the Bay of Biscay. The church in Vitoria, south of San Sebastian, welcomed us, and Eibar, a small town in a mountainous region, received the Word with gladness.

Once again, there was a tremendous need for good teaching on divine healing, Bible prosperity, and our identity in Christ. We followed the Holy Spirit in ministering to the people with the laying on of hands and the prophetic gift.

One dear pastor, originally from Finland, was so upset that the word *rich* was in the Bible. We gently tried to instruct him from the Bible the truth and meaning of the word *rich* and how wonderful that God provided for His children to live in such a way that all of our needs are met and we can have much more in order to support the Gospel and be generous to others. Then he proceeded to tell us he was in the process of building a retirement home in a beautiful area of Spain. We thought to ourselves, "You must have money to build a retirement home."

Denmark

During the summer of 1991, while preaching in an African church in Paris, we were introduced to a pastor from Horsens, Denmark. He invited us to minister in his church. When November arrived, we were on our way to Denmark from Gatwick Airport in England to Billund, Denmark, the home of Legoland. The topography of the land is quite flat, dotted with a variety of thatched roof farmhouses intermingled among the modern homes along the way. The cold damp winter weather welcomed us, but was soon overcome by the love and warmth of Pastors Johannes and Aase Muhlig at Rhema Church. Their hospitality was first class.

The people loved the Word of God and welcomed us to minister as the Holy Spirit led. Johannes was instrumental in doors opening to churches in other cities, such as Aarhus, Odense, and Esbjerg. We returned many times to preach and teach with glorious results. I ministered in a Women's Aglow meeting in Horsens.

Johannes had been in the printing business and offered to re-print Gordon's book, *What On Earth Are You Saying?*, as well as translations in Danish and French. He also arranged for my first books to be printed in English, *Let Patience Work for You* and *Seeking and Finding the Good Life*. What a rich blessing the Lord gave us through these servants of the Lord.

Holland

Our dear friend, Pastor Keith Stuarte, who is now pastoring in Waterbury, Connecticut, contacted us inquiring as to whether we would like to go to Holland. He recommended us to many churches under the leadership of Johan Maasbach in The Hague.

More Open Doors of Ministry in Europe

In 1958, in the Malieveld, The Hague, a large crusade took place under the ladership of evangelist T.L. Osborn, with Johan Maasbach as his interpreter. It was a revival Holland had never experienced before. This was a great breakthrough for the full Gospel in Holland. From that time on, Johan Maasbach traveled through Holland and all over the world to organize crusades and preach the Gospel of Jesus Christ. By the grace of God, many Pentecostal churches were founded, and numerous people got saved through the ministry of the Johan Maasbach World Mission Foundation (Maasbach Radio).

In August of 1991, we began a wonderful series of meetings in nine cities in the beautiful nation of Holland and one in Belgium, under Johan Maasbach's ministry.

The Lord connected us with a sister in Belgium, who arranged for us to hold a conference in the north of Holland in the winter of 1998 in the town of Veeningen. Despite the freezing cold weather, the meetings were well attended at The White Fields Conference Center. The people gladly received the Word, and we were able to make available a number of our books, which had been translated and printed into the Dutch language.

Much later, in the fall of 2005, we ministered in Delft, a beautiful city with numerous canals. We have never seen so many bicycles in one place! The pastors, David and Melanie Koerts, and their church gladly received the ministry of the Word and the manifestation of the gifts of the Holy Spirit.

During the weekend we visited Delft it was a joy to connect with my sister Elizabeth who was visiting her son, Erik, and his family who were living in a nearby town. They all joined us for the Sunday morning service. It was such a delight to have family around us.

First Tour to Israel

It is only a four-hour flight to Israel from London, making it quite accessible for Europeans to visit. An invitation was extended to us to join another ministry in November of 1998.

Our base was in Bethlehem, and our accommodation at the Bethlehem Hotel in the center of town was clean and comfortable. Each morning, we joined our tour guide to various sites from Jerusalem to Jericho, the Dead Sea, the Sea of Galilee, and other historic towns.

On our last night in Bethlehem, Gordon arranged to hold a meeting in one of the hotel rooms, inviting all in our tour group. News spread that we were having a meeting and others joined us.

Gordon preached with authority and a strong anointing, inviting those who wanted us to pray for them to come forward. The response brought many who desired healing and ministry in the prophetic. While dining, we noticed an attractive lady in the dining room, not part of our group, and she was among those attending our meeting. She came forward for prayer. We ministered to her after confirming she knew Jesus as her Lord and

Savior. Then we instructed her how to receive the baptism in the Holy Spirit, and then the Lord had an encouraging word for her. As she was about to give us her business card, two body guards stopped her. Who was this woman of seeming prominence?

This lovely lady was the mother-in-law of Yasser Arafat, who at the time was head of the Palestinian authority. It was so amazing that God brought her to the meeting that night. The Lord knows how to minister to those in places of position. Raymonda Tawil was definitely in the right place at the right time. We believe the Holy Spirit did a work in her that night, and only eternity will reveal the rest of the story.

Switzerland

As a result of ministering at a church in Saint-Gaudens, in the south of France, we were invited to minister in the beautiful country of Switzerland. The day came when we flew into Geneva during the month of May 1993. About an hour's drive away, we arrived in Écublens on Lake Geneva.

The Lord always prepared us for each meeting where we ministered. Most of the time it was plowing and allowing the Holy Spirit to wash away the traditions of men and religion. The Lord had told us many years before that nothing could stand before His Word; no culture, no religion, and no man's tradition. We were confident in the Lord that His Word would never return void.

We ministered in this church on two visits with manifestations of the Holy Spirit and anointed teaching. The people lacked teaching and understanding in the area of the finished work of Christ and who they are in Him. The joy of the Lord was lacking through their ignorance of the truth. They were not speaking in line with the Word of God.

One area that held the people in bondage was the seeming need for deliverance over and over again. The church was ready with plenty of paper towels to assist those who vomited up the demons. We ignored this and kept on preaching and teaching the truth and believed some received revelation knowledge of their place and authority in Jesus.

One lady was upset with me, telling me the broach I was wearing was evil. In love, I gently taught her it meant nothing, and there was no demon power in this piece of jewelry. You can hardly believe what some Christians are taught to believe as Gospel truth without searching the Scriptures.

On the practical side of our visit, we were driven up into the beautiful Swiss Alps to visit the town of Gruyere, known for its delicious cheese. The many herds of cows pasturing along the roadway provided this gourmet food. The Swiss food for the most part is organic and healthy. There is delicious Swiss chocolate too.

During the 1980's, while living in California, we hosted several foreign students in our home for short visits as they attended a local university to learn English. Among the students, we were happy to welcome two young men, one from Germany and the other from Switzerland. The Lord opened Andre's heart and he received Jesus as His Savior in our home. I remembered he lived in Switzerland and we contacted him while we were there. He attended one of our meetings, and it was a great joy to see him going on with the Lord.

Even before the Lord released us to the nations, we were ministering to foreign students in our home. This included two young ladies from Japan and the other from Indonesia.

Scotland

My maternal grandfather's family came from Scotland, and they were called Ulster-Scots. My ancestral history was of great interest to me when we were invited to minister in the town of Dunblane not far from the historic city of Edinburgh. The people in the church needed much encouragement and healing from a painful tragedy that affected the whole town.

In 1996, there had been the deadliest mass murder of sixteen children in a primary school in the town. It shocked the nation. We relied heavily on the Holy Spirit to minister deeply into the hearts of the people. So many had been affected by this tragic loss of life. Jesus is still a Healing Jesus.

Scotland is a beautiful country, and every moment was immensely enjoyed as we were taken to St. Andrews on the North Sea, the home of golf. When the pastor heard my Giffin family roots were from Scotland, he graciously drove us to the town of Beith where there are only a few remains of the little castle named after the family. Today there is a mansion named Giffin House, a tourist guest house. Another memorable visit was to Loch Lomond where we enjoyed a boat ride over the beautiful Loch.

Ireland

Our first ministry to the Emerald Isle was in May, 2007. A church in a suburb of Dublin opened their doors for us to minister. We were graciously hosted by Pastors Paul and Caroline Perry at Cornerstone Church. It was a blessed weekend of ministry to a diverse congregation. Since Ireland belongs to the European Union, there has been an influx of people moving to Ireland from Poland and other Eastern European countries. The Word was received, and the people were uplifted through the teaching and ministry in the gifts of the Holy Spirit. It was a grand weekend with our lovely Irish friends.

We had the pleasure of enjoying a train ride down the coastline from the Blackrock train station, taking in the beautiful Irish seascape. Catching our attention were the Irish houses decorated with such colorful doors. Even the mail boxes are green, matching the lush verdant hills.

Chapter 19

South America is Calling

The eight hour flight from Lisbon via Porto was nearing its destination to São Paulo, Brazil. Our day began at London's Heathrow airport where we caught a flight to Lisbon in June of 1997. After a brief stopover in this beautiful city, it was time to board the next leg of our journey to South America. The plane was sparsely filled, so we had a few seats to stretch out and be comfortable on the night flight.

The month of June is the beginning of summer in England, whereas autumn greeted us as we landed early the following day in the large metropolis of Sãn Paulo. Heavy rains proceeded us as evidenced by slight flooding on the streets, and the overcast sky promised more rain.

We were warmly greeted by a brother from one of the main Four Square Pentecostal churches in the city. He whisked us away through the streets, teaming with fast moving traffic, as we moved to the center of the city. A pleasant room in a nice hotel had been booked, and we soon settled in, taking a much-needed rest after the long journey. The gift of a beautiful bouquet of red roses made the room feel warm and welcoming.

It can take a few days to acclimate to the time change and jet lag. The next morning, an early phone call notified us that we would be picked up and taken to a church to minister. We followed directions as the host church had our schedule well planned to minister in many churches.

We soon found the people of Brazil warm and hungry for the things of God and the Holy Spirit. Morning meetings in the middle of the week were well attended. We experienced a glorious move of God on our first ministry trip to Brazil. We saw firsthand the excitement and enthusiasm of a great land where churches are open and flourishing nearly every day and evening. Mothers held their babies and often stood two to three hours because of the crowded churches. The churches boldly minister the Word of God on radio and television, resulting in the Spirit of the Lord sweeping away religion and darkness. It wasn't unusual for us to minister at two churches in one evening.

While in Sãn Paulo, we had the privilege of ministering on radio and television. Many were saved and healed as the Gospel went forth in every meeting. The prophetic word, ministered through the anointing of the Holy Spirit, lifted the people with much encouragement and comfort. It was so wonderful to see how valuable and priceless the gift of prophecy flowing through our ministry affected whole congregations and hundreds of pastors and church leaders. They stood in awe as the Holy Spirit demonstrated His mighty power in most unusual ways and manifestations.

It is difficult to describe the love and warmth one feels from the Brazilian people, a land of great contrasts of rich and poor. Like most world cities, there is violence, tragedy, and heart-ache. On the other hand, there is love, wonderful worship, and a great moving of the Spirit of God for those who desire Him. Jesus is indeed very present and near to the people of Brazil.

It was such a joy to minister at a Four Square ministers conference in the beautiful Serra Negra mountains outside of Sãn Paulo. The conference venue is located in a beautiful setting with many coffee plantations surrounding it.

We recall how hungry the pastors were for the Word of God and the prophetic ministry. At our last meeting, we ministered to nearly three hundred pastors in the prophetic with mighty manifestations and demonstrations in the Spirit. It was not only amazing to the pastors but to us as well. There was such a strong anointing, and the Holy Spirit strengthened us to flow with Him.

The city of Sãn Paulo is teaming with millions of people. The streets are crowded, even in the residential areas. One evening, we were driven to a meeting by one of the pastors, maneuvering much too fast we thought, as many people and children were milling around the sidewalks and streets. Suddenly our driver hit a young boy, and he bounced off the hood of the car. Stunned, he quickly got up off the ground, and his mother ran to him. It was quite disturbing to see this accident, and we promptly prayed for him, believing he was all right and God's healing power ministered to him. The pastor gave his mother money to take him to the doctor. It was a shock to us to witness an accident that could have been prevented. We leaned heavily on the Holy Spirit to help us focus on the ministry that night.

Nearing the end of our ministry, the Brazilian people were filled with passion and excitement as their soccer team was playing against France in the final game of the World Cup in Paris. After church on Sunday, we were taken to a pastor's home where we watched the game. Along the way, people were not to be found on the streets, not even a dog. Everyone was glued to their televisions. The Brazilians were getting ready to party that night; they were sure their team would win the World Cup. Oh, but the disappointment was painful when France won. Soccer is big in South American countries.

There is no shortage of good beef and other meats in Brazil. We were often treated to meals at the Churrascaria restaurants. The delicious beef and other meats such as pork, lamb, chicken or duck were brought to our table and served by a meat waiter, *passadores*, who freshly sliced it from the skewer with a large knife and served it on our plates. All the meats were roasted with either wood or charcoal. What a special treat!

One evening while dining at one large churrascaria, Gordon and I were treated to special live romantic Brazilian music and dancing in honor of our thirty-fourth wedding anniversary. The Brazilians know how to celebrate!

The following year we returned to Brazil during the month of August, ministering in many of the same churches as well as new ones.

Chapter 20

Moving to the Country

In 1994, we were led to move from Putney, in southwest London, to the county of Surrey, situated about thirty miles south of London. The task of looking for accommodation began with excitement. We found a farm cottage in the picturesque village of Bramley, nearby the prestigious city of Guildford. It was just what we needed, a quiet little house secluded and quaint on farmland. The owner, a gentleman farmer who lived nearby raised cows. We enjoyed seeing the newly birthed calves grazing with their mothers in the pasture, each one labeled with their own name. Often the deer fed close by in the early morning mist and red foxes appeared regularly near the house. It was an extremely peaceful place to rest and prepare for international ministry trips.

We soon outgrew this delightful little English farm cottage and the search was on for larger accommodation. The result was The Lodge on the other side of Guildford in the village of Send. The Lodge, a Victorian Grade II listed home dating back to 1871, belonged to the lady who owned the palatial Manor House down the lane. In days gone by, The Lodge was the home of the gardener-maintenance person. It perfectly met our needs. Now we were challenged to believe God for the increased rent, double from what we had been paying. We stretched our faith and expected the Lord to faithfully come through. God favored us with the owner, although she had doubts we might not be able to pay the rent!

On our return from a ministry trip in Belgium we picked up our mail and sure enough, there was a sizeable check waiting for us, more than enough to pay the first month's rent and a deposit. We soon moved into the historic Victorian lodge, surrounded by a typical English country garden and a small decorative fish pond near the back door of the conservatory. English country living suited us to the tea. It provided hospitality for our guests, including barbeques and English cream teas. Our friends and overseas visitors were delighted to visit us. We had access to the many country walks along the public footpaths, and towpaths along the nearby river Wey, a tributary of the Thames River, a popular river for vacation boats to meander through the beautiful countryside. Bordering the back yard of the home was a screened tall fence, protecting us from the hard cricket balls during cricket season. A few escaped the fence and landed on the roof of the house. The local Send cricket club played over the summer months with serious competition from other clubs.

By the way, we never missed paying the rent on time!

Our Thirtieth Wedding Anniversary

Shortly after moving into The Lodge in 1994, our Thirtieth Wedding Anniversary was approaching on August 19, 1994. We strongly desired to host a memorable celebration, inviting our children, family, and friends.

Our twenty-fifth Anniversary was only attended by my sister, Elizabeth and her husband John, while we lived in London. We began to search for a suitable venue in the beautiful Surrey countryside. Not far away, in the village of Ockham we found a country hotel and restaurant, The Hautboy, an interesting mid-nineteenth-century building. It was a charming Victorian structure with mock Tudor windows and adorned with quatrefoils (four-petal flowers). This perfectly suited us for this happy celebration.

Several of our wedding party attended. Rev Peter Douglas, who gave me away on my wedding day, Marion Clark (Hall), maid of honor and bridesmaids, Pamela Croft (Spurdle) and Ruth Treadaway (Rupniak). Rev Selwyn Hughes, who officiated at our wedding, was unable to attend, but he sent us loving congratulations.

Jason and Zoe flew in from California. It was a special reunion for the cousins.

God Sends us Help

We soon met a dear lady who became such a precious friend to us. She made herself available to help us in the administrative side of the ministry by doing our bookkeeping and serving us with many practical skills. Margret Gilder shared this testimony with us, and it will bless you as you read what the Lord did in her life through the ministry.

Margaret Gilder's Testimony

It was over twenty years ago that I first met Gordon and Barbara White. My brother invited me to one of their meetings in Guildford, Surrey. I felt the warmth of the love of God; I knew I was with God's people, and it brought a feeling of love and acceptance.

After a short time I started to help with their accounts. This brought us close together as friends. It was during one of these visits that I was asked if I would like to be baptized in the Holy Spirit and pray in tongues. What happened next was amazing. I accepted Jesus as my Savior as a child, but up to this time, I did not know about this wonderful gift. After Gordon and Barbara prayed for me, I received the baptism in the Holy Spirit and began speaking in tongues. We looked up from where we were seated in the conservatory of their home, and a beautiful white dove landed in their garden pond at that special moment. How wonderful it was! My life has never been the same.

I began to understand how much God loves me and how to love and forgive others. What a change in my life because of the teachings from the Word of God, I received through Gordon and Barbara. I know what they say is what they live by.

I joined them in travelling to many places. God enriched my life on the ministry journeys to Bermuda and Israel. In Bermuda, I helped Barbara hold a woman's conference. That was wonderful. What fun we had meeting so many lovely Bermudians and American friends of Gordon and Barbara.

Meetings were held in Wimbledon, England, on many occasions. On one occasion, a party of ladies came over from Georgia and held an Eagle's Wings Women's conference. What a blessing they were to me and many other people. That time was wonderful; they not only worshiped but reached out to the people in and around Wimbledon and went to London where they showed God's love to the people they met in the streets and restaurants. I wanted to be part of this wonderful love they were showing me. To this day, I try hard to show this same wonderful love to those I come in contact with.

I am always so happy to stay in their home, sharing all that God has given them. I feel so at home with them; they certainly are true friends. What they say is what they truly mean. A saying is: "True friend's are like diamonds, precious and rare, but false friends are like autumn leaves that can be found everywhere." I have found this to be true in my life. So I praise God for pointing me to Barbara and Gordon whom I call my true friends. I love you both.

Life of Faith Fellowship

While living in the Guildford area, the Lord provided a wonderful group of believers who surrounded us in prayer and financial support. From time to time, we hosted meetings at the YMCA in the center of the city where God moved wonderfully by His Spirit. We sensed the need of establishing a church where these people could come together and be taught the Word of God as there was not a church at that time that preached the revelation truths from the New Testament on faith, healing, and prosperity. The next step was finding a suitable location to meet regularly on a Sunday morning.

A new theatre opened by the Wey River right in the center of this historic town called *The Electric Theatre*, so named as the building had been used by the electric company in former years. It seemed to be the perfect place, with a meeting room upstairs. We began meetings in 1997.

We established a wonderful relationship with two of the women attending and assisting us. It wasn't long before we observed God's call upon their lives, and we knew we were to encourage and mentor them in their ministry. Barb Witt and Mieke Colleé faithfully served the Lord in various aspects of ministry and were seasoned in the Word of God, both of whom travelled with us to Bermuda and to Lanzarote in the Canary Islands. Mieke accompanied us to Amsterdam to help with Faith Women of Europe Conference in 2000. A group of ladies in Brussels, Belgium hosted Faith Women of Europe the year before.

Mieke Colleé's Testimony

I met Barbara at an afternoon gathering where she was the speaker. It was a defining moment in my life. The clarity of the Word she shared and faith in that Word impacted me.

A couple of days later, Gordon and Barbara ministered to me prophetically with accuracy and authority at one of their meetings in Guildford. This was at an evening meeting in January 1997. In February, they started a church, Life of Faith Fellowship, in Guildford, Surrey. I knew I was going to be part of it. It was a spiritual home where the word of faith was being preached, and the gifts of the Holy Spirit were exercised with integrity.

Gordon and Barbara were great encouragers and allowed the gifts that God had deposited in me to be brought out and flourish. I came under a canopy of a ministry of excellence. They were such a beautiful example. We all flowed together in unity, allowing God to be first in our lives.

It was such a blessing to be part of Faith Ministries International, and the Faith Women of Europe Conferences in England, the Netherlands, Belgium, and Bermuda.

I grew spiritually, traveled with them, witnessed miracles, and had the joy of being ordained under their ministry. But above all, we became and always will be the closest of friends and prayer partners, which I know God ordained before the foundation of the world. I thank God for Gordon and Barbara.

I was led to hold Faith Women meetings once a month at The Electric Theater and invited guest speakers to bless the women with anointed teaching. Opportunities opened to hold Faith Woman of Europe seminars in Guildford, Birmingham, Reading, Worthing, and Wimbledon.

The Life of Faith Fellowship in Guildford, Surrey, was moving forward with a faithful core group of believers, intercessors, and financial support. We felt it was time to ordain Barb Witt and Mieke Colleé at one of the Sunday morning services.

Barb Witt's Testimony

I first came to know about Brother Gordon and Barbara and Faith Ministries International when they came as guest speakers to the church I attended in London in 1989. They returned a few months later and announced they had moved from California to England.

As there was very little access to faith teaching in the United Kingdom, I immediately signed up for their mailing list and began to attend their meetings. As soon as I received a letter from them, I immediately went to the calendar and marked the date for the next meeting. I looked forward to it for weeks in advance.

I can remember standing out in the freezing cold weather many times, waiting for a train to Guildford or somewhere else to attend their meetings. Eventually, they approached me about helping them in some capacity in their meetings. I was so honored that they asked me, and I offered to greet people and generally do anything necessary. In the years they were in the United Kingdom, I only ever missed one of their meetings.

When Brother Gordon told me they were going to start a church in Guildford, I told him I would be there to help. All during this time, I was continuing in the study of the Word, gradually learning the principles of Bible faith. As I became more involved in the ministry, I had a desire to move out of London to what Barbara called, "the well-watered, fruitful, abundant, prosperous land of Surrey."

It was a big step of faith for me, and I sowed seed into Faith Ministries International, believing God to meet all my needs. One day, I received a phone call from Brother Gordon and Barbara, saying they had seen an advertisement for an apartment, and they thought I should come and look at it. They met me at the train station and took me to view it. It was brand new! I moved in shortly afterward.

I still remember when Barbara asked me to speak at one of her Faith Women of Europe meetings. I was so honored, and I didn't even have to think about what I was going to speak on. I already knew – How to Change Things.

From that point on, they began to give me opportunities in church to receive the tithes and offerings. I had of necessity become a student of the Word in that area. I can speak from personal experience – the Word works. Other opportunities to teach the Word in church came forth when they would be away traveling.

On one occasion, the next morning at breakfast, after I had spent the night at their home after returning late from one of their meetings, Brother Gordon mentioned to me that they wanted to ordain me into the ministry. I think it was such a shock to me that it took a while for it to sink in. It was indeed a special occasion and one that I will never forget.

I probably would not be in the ministry today if it had not been for Brother Gordon and Barbara. They were strong and spiritually secure ministers, who were not afraid to give me opportunities that I probably would never have been given anywhere else in the United Kingdom.

> For this I will always be grateful. I believe they also planted many spiritual seeds in the UK, and many prophetic words have gone forth over my life and over the nation through Faith Ministries International that are in the process of being fulfilled.
>
> As Brother Gordon used to say, "God said it – I believe it!"

My Miracle of Healing

One Sunday at Life of Faith Fellowship, we had a visit from a couple we had met while teaching at a Bible School in Ramsey, Cambridgeshire. It was so difficult for the wife to get up the stairs as she arrived in a wheel chair due to surgery on her head as a result of a brain tumor. She persevered that day and was not disappointed. Anne Graham's testimony is amazing.

> After my husband Peter and I moved to Cyprus, I was diagnosed with a massive brain tumor, and I had to be brought back to the United Kingdom for an operation in Southampton General Hospital.

The tumor was so large, that it had put its roots right into my skull. The doctor had to cut part of my skull away to get at the roots, removing what they could. I was so damaged that I lost the complete use of my left side. I could not walk or use my left arm or hand. My speech was affected, and I had palsy of the face. The optic nerves in both eyes were damaged so that I could not read my Bible, watch television, or see people clearly because of the double vision.

The hospital told my husband Peter I would never be able to walk again, and I would need constant supervision. The eye hospital said I should register as blind as I would not be able to see properly again. This meant a monetary allowance, but we declined and believed God for my healing.

It is fortunate I had been diligent in reading my Bible and learning healing Scriptures because the Holy Spirit brought them to mind while I lay there in the hospital for eight months. Peter and I stayed fixed on God's Word being true and that He would heal me. I kept speaking healing Scriptures over my life.

I finally returned to our home in Southsea, a ground floor flat, as I was in a wheelchair. Then we encountered the problem of finding a church that was moving in the Holy Spirit. The first place we attended was a Full Gospel Businessmen's dinner in Southsea. The speaker, who had a healing ministry, prayed for me. From that moment on, there was a marked improvement in my health.

Shortly thereafter, we visited Gordon and Barbara White's church, Life of Faith Fellowship in Guildford, Surrey. We had met the Whites a few years previous when they ministered at a Bible college in Ramsey, Cambridgeshire. It was dreadfully difficult for Peter to take me into the church as it was upstairs, but we persevered. After Gordon and Barbara and the congregation prayed for me, I was able to walk down the stairs backward, holding the rail with my right hand. From that moment on, I got stronger and stronger. Each week, I came under the anointing in the services, and there was a marked improvement. When I attended the ladies' meeting, Faith Women of Europe, I was ministered to again, and continued to get stronger and stronger. By this time, my eyesight had improved, and I was able to read my Bible again. At church, I didn't have to come down the stairs backward. I walked forward with a full cup of coffee in my hand!

Think about it – the hospital could do nothing for me after the operation. But God moved my brain back into place. The eye specialist admitted that God had done more for me than they could. I have only two percent of my eyesight to go. Praise God, I am even driving the car now.

So I give all the glory to God. As it says in Psalm 103:2-3, "Bless the Lord Oh my soul and all that is within me, Bless His holy name," I will not forget all His benefits. He has forgiven all my iniquities, and healed all my diseases.

The Hundredfold Return

Gordon and I purposed to be diligent in teaching the whole counsel of God. The Gospel of the Lord Jesus Christ encompasses everything Jesus bought and paid for with His precious Blood, ushering in a new and better covenant.

Poverty is included in the curse of the law (Deuteronomy 28), from which we have been redeemed just as truly as we have been redeemed from our sins, diseases, and sicknesses. Jesus said that those who give up all to follow him, including giving up houses, lands, and family for the sake of the Gospel would receive a vast return, even a hundredfold now in this life. Sometimes we overlook the word *persecutions*. Nevertheless, persecutions will come but we are not to be disturbed. We are overcomers in Christ.

> "And Jesus answered and said, Verily I say unto you, There is no man that hath left house, or brethren, or sisters, or father, or mother, or wife, or children, or lands, for my sake, and the gospel's, But he shall receive an hundredfold now in this time, houses, and brethren, and sisters, and mothers, and children, and lands, with persecutions; and in the world to come eternal life." (Mark 10:29-30)

While ministering at a Brazilian church in London one Sunday, we made our books available for purchase at the end of the service. A young man expressed the desire to purchase the books, but he didn't have the money on him that day. As I listened to the Holy Spirit, He said to sow these books into his life. We often gave our books away.

We never thought any more about what happened that day, but God never forgets or neglects to honor the seeds we plant. One day, a few years later, we had an e-mail from the brother to whom we had given the books. To our surprise, God had mightily blessed him in the financial area, and he wanted to sow into the ministry £1,000. He told us that this represented the one hundredfold return on what we had sown into his life a few years previously.

You can imagine our delight in hearing how God had prospered this brother in the Lord. We quickly replied to the email, giving him the necessary bank information he needed to make the deposit. From that time on, this brother continues to sow into the ministry. Our Father God is utterly faithful to bring to pass His covenant provisions.

A Different Story in Wales

The measure of Bible teaching you receive and believe makes all the difference in the way you perceive God's material and financial blessings. Everything God has revealed to us in His Word must be personally received by revelation of the Holy Spirit to make it active and working in our lives. We can't live successfully off someone else's revelation. This definitely applies in the area of financial and material blessings.

At a church in South Wales, we poured out our hearts as we ministered the Word to the people. The spiritual temperature was low and the people were bound by religious traditions. As usual, we ignored the atmosphere and preached what the Holy Spirit desired the people to hear.

When we entered the church a man was quite upset with us and loudly spoke these words in our presence, "The Apostle Paul would never have driven a car like that!"

Our first thought was, "Well, the Apostle Paul didn't have the opportunity to drive a car, they hadn't been invented. But he did ride on donkeys, and the best that was available in his day, and he even sailed on ships as he preached the gospel".

We didn't respond. Out of his heart and spiritual ignorance this man spoke loud and clear his misguided information. Gordon and I never compromised when it came to teaching Bible prosperity for we knew the people needed to hear the Word so that faith could come. When faith and revelation come the people position themselves to receive the blessings already provided for them. Poverty is a curse and it is also a spirit that blinds and binds God's people.

God had blessed us with a good, comfortable, high-end car to carry His Word to the people. Now isn't that a wonderful blessing? Never compromise and apologize for the goodness and blessings of the Lord.

Miracle Children

Among the many dear people who attended our meetings in London and Guildford, both at the YMCA and Life of Faith Fellowship, was a young couple from London. James and Bola Ashaye had only been married for six years, and they had a strong desire to have children. Our relationship with James and Bola grew over the years and they affectionately called Gordon "Daddy" and me "Mummy". They still call me "Mummy."

The following testimony will rejoice your heart in the miracle working power of our God.

> We regularly attended Faith Ministries International meetings and churches in the London area when we heard Gordon and Barbara were ministering.
>
> The doctor's tests confirmed that my sperm count was low. This added to our disappointment on not having conceived. When we consulted the doctor, he suggested in vitro fertilization (IVF). Just before the IVF treatment began, my wife conceived! When the test was carried out, it was revealed that it was an ectopic pregnancy, meaning the conception took place

in the fallopian tube, not the uterus. The doctor advised us to terminate the pregnancy due to endangering my wife's life.

Just after this heartbreaking news, we attended a Faith Ministries International meeting in Guildford in 1997. Daddy White prophesied with a message in tongues, and Mummy interpreted the message. I recorded it on a tape so that we could pray over these powerful words from the Lord. The Lord said that He would make all the necessary adjustments, and things will slide into the appropriate position, and that God would help us.

It was after we heard and received the prophecy that we told them our problem. They agreed with us in prayer. Three days after the prophecy was given, we went back to the consultant to terminate the pregnancy, but not before another ultra sound was taken. The scan revealed that God had moved the baby from the fallopian tube into the uterus where the baby should be! Glory to God!

The consultant was greatly shocked, as you can imagine, and said there is no medical explanation to justify what had happened. Our perfect baby boy, Joshua, was delivered at full term. Today he is studying medicine at the University College London. He has won several academic awards because he is such an extremely brilliant child.

Two years after Joshua was born, God gave us our daughter, Maria, who is now in higher school. This is how God used Gordon and Barbara White to deliver us from bareness through the faith and the prophetic word. Isn't God good?

There were other numerous occasions when these special people of God have prophetically spoken into our lives. None of them have failed to come to pass. They were pointedly accurate, and God used them to reveal deep and secret things to us too numerous to mention.

How we miss Daddy Gordon!
James and Bola Ashaye

Chapter 21

A New Millenium — A Change in Direction

Gordon and I were accustomed to change. We learned over the years to remain secure and steady when the Lord gave us new directions. We purposed to always stay in agreement as we followed the leading of the Holy Spirit. The year 2000 would be no different. In fact, it was a pivotal point in our life and ministry.

The year began with many plans. Included in our itinerary was the excitement of leading a ministry tour to Israel in April. We invited our long time ministry friend, Peter Douglas, to help us and extended the invitation to Pastors Paul and Nancy Glass of Rex World Outreach in Atlanta to join us, along with members of their congregation. Our group was mightily blessed as our tour guide Joni Arden skillfully led us through the many Biblical sites with precise knowledge and great humor.

On our return to England after a blessed and successful ministry tour in Israel, we prepared for a Faith Women of Europe seminar in Amsterdam, Holland. The Lord had raised up a team of wonderful women to arrange these meetings, including Maria Rossi, our interpreter from Belgium. Mieke Colleé accompanied us from England. The meetings flowed in the anointing of the Holy Spirit and women's lives were transformed through anointed teaching.

It wasn't long afterwards, around the beginning of May, we were packing again for a trip back to the USA via Toronto where we visited my brother Elden, his wife Isabel, and their family. Our next stop would be San Francisco. For some time, Gordon felt he would be ministering in that area, and now was the time. It was a fruitful and blessed ministry, the beginning of many other ministry opportunities in that area.

When the Lord prepares you for change there is always a stirring in your spirit signaling you to be alert and listen inwardly to His direction. It was a gradual change but with great peace and assurance from the Word of God.

One day, we were enjoying a time of fellowship with a dear Pastor from London, Roger Stedman, a trusted brother in the Lord. As we shared things on our heart, he spoke prophetically into our lives, and it confirmed what the Lord was saying to us. Among other things the Lord emphasized through him that "our children needed us." At the time, it seemed strange to hear these words, seeing our children were grown up and on their own and two were married. They were seemingly doing well, including their spiritual lives. We did not dismiss the words, but we knew the Lord would reveal to us exactly what He was talking about.

How awesome is the Holy Spirit–He said He would "show us things to come" (John 16:13). God's Word never generates fear but always a quiet assurance and preparation in our hearts to move forward and make decisions based on His Word and His peace in our hearts.

By the time August arrived, we knew in our spirits exactly what we were to do and it was the most natural and spiritual thing to relocate to California. We had a home awaiting us. The Lord had provided this home for us in 1995, a place for us to live whenever we returned to California. The next step was to sell our furniture in England and make all the necessary preparations. We were on the move once again, not with sadness or regrets, but with an inner excitement and joy.

We prayed, "Lord, what do you really have planned for us in this new venture?" Our lives had always been an adventure as we followed the Holy Spirit. We never had frets or regrets along the way, which would be such a waste of time and energy when we knew in our spirits that He always leads perfectly and precisely at the right time.

The boxes were packed, and the moving company came to arrange shipment back to the United States. It was quite supernatural to see how quickly the furniture sold; many other things were given away. We were ready to fly back to California. How quickly every detail came together.

On October 23rd, 2000, we were met by our daughter Zoe at the Los Angeles airport with great excitement. It didn't take long to get settled into our home and seek the Lord for His direction concerning ministry. We took advantage of a short season of adjustment and rest after laboring in many nations of the world for twelve years.

We knew our international ministry had not been completed. In the meantime, we sought the Lord for a home church that taught the Word of God. The Lord led us to Foothill Family Church in Lake Forest where we sat under the anointed teaching of Pastor Mike Webb. This is still my home church.

A year after our return to Corona, we were aware of how much our children needed us to be near them. Even as adults, they encountered challenges that were extremely difficult for a time. We stood with them and assisted where necessary and saw God faithfully bring them through tough and stressful times.

The spring of 2002 was approaching, and we joyfully looked forward to the marriage of our oldest son Jason to Michelle Costa. It was a beautiful wedding in Santa Barbara, overlooking the Pacific Ocean. Gordon and I had the privilege of performing the ceremony.

In October of that year, Gordon and I were gathered together with our daughter Zoe in our living room on a Monday morning, praying for the ministry and other needs. Gordon was reading Psalm 103 when he suddenly turned ashen and temporarily passed out. I quickly put my hands on him and in the Name of Jesus took authority over the attack on his body. Zoe ran to the phone and called 911. I knew what the enemy was trying to do and was aware that he had had a heart attack. Quickly the paramedics arrived and persuaded Gordon to go to the hospital to be tested. He thought he had just fainted. Sure enough it was a heart attack, which necessitated a four way bypass surgery at Loma Linda Hospital that week. Praise God, Gordon made a wonderful recovery and was fit enough to travel overseas for ministry the following March. I believe this surgery prolonged Gordon's life for another twelve years.

Gordon was interested in finding our friend, Dr. Joe Poppell. We had not seen him since his ministry with us in Stewart Baptist Church in Georgia in the 1970's. Gordon did a little research with the help of information in the back of Joe's book. With a phone call to Georgia he found out Joe was living in Palm Springs.

We found his address and promptly visited him. This was the beginning of a time of precious fellowship in the Lord for the next twelve years. When Gordon went to be with the Lord, Joe sent me this loving tribute that I share with you:

Dr. Joe Poppell

Brother Gordon White was a special friend of mine for many years, – who I appreciated very much. My words are insufficient to describe my thoughts and feelings toward this great man of God. I saw him as a man of faith, a man of integrity, and a man who would go above and beyond what was expected of him. His eyes were upon the Lord, and his heart was full of the Word of God. To have a conversation with him was to see the better side of things. He was very positive and a man of quality, which is hard to duplicate. He was a true friend, who was a great blessing to my family and me.

A few months after Gordon was promoted to heaven, our dear Brother Joe followed him into glory. I know they are having the time of their life walking the streets of gold with Jesus.

We received another powerful testimony from Deborah Alexander. God will meet you right where you are when you are hungry.

My Encounter with the Holy Spirit

While I was employed at a fitness gym in Norco, California, I met three people whom God used to change my life. In July 2001, Gordon and Barbara White and their daughter Zoe started coming on a regular basis. I soon found out how much they loved the Lord, and at every opportunity I would talk to them about the Word of God. I had many questions, and it wasn't long until Gordon and Barbara were telling me about the baptism in the Holy Spirit and how I, as a believer, should receive this wonderful gift. They taught me how the Holy Spirit would give me power and help me in my prayer life.

I became hungrier for the things of God. I sought every opportunity to learn more about how to receive this gift. One day I took a break from my work and asked Gordon and Barbara to come with me to the broom closet, so they could pray for me in private. Right there in the middle of all the mops, brooms, and cleaning supplies, they laid hands on me. It was amazing! The power of God started to move from the bottom of my stomach and then up to my mouth, and I began to speak in tongues. At first I wondered if this was real, but as I continued to pray in tongues, there was a greater release, and I knew it was true. I know the baptism in the Holy Spirit is real, as Jesus said in His Word in John 7:38, "He that believeth on me, as the scripture hath said, out of his belly shall flow rivers of living water."

I started to receive wonderful answers to prayer. God continues to do amazing things in my life and leads me by His Spirit and the Word of God. Jesus will meet you wherever you are – even in the broom closet! Just be hungry and receive all He has provided for you in His Word.

Family Miracle in 2013

How much the Lord loves and cares for our families. This is a recent testimony to God's healing and miracle working power in the life of our precious grandson, Seth. The grace and goodness of God is awesome!

Our Son's Miracle-Perry and Zoe Parris

My husband and I were delightfully surprised when we found out we were having a baby. Our son, Seth, is a special gift from the Lord. He definitely is an "appointed one", as his name means. We saw God's blessing on his life from birth.

During November 2013, Seth, at the age of six years old, started complaining of headaches. At first we thought it could either be an allergy, head cold, or sinus infection. When the head pains did not go away, we took him to his pediatrician to find out what the problem was. The first diagnosis the doctor said was probably a sinus infection, but if the pain did not go away to be sure and bring Seth back.

We continued to pray for him as we know that Jesus is still a Healer, and healing belongs to us today. We knew it wasn't normal for a six year old to have so many headaches. We continued to observe him from day to day. The headaches continued and became more severe. In the space of five days, we took him back to the doctor three times. On the second visit, an eye exam was ordered. On the third visit, blood work was ordered.

On December 17, the fourth visit, we saw an after-hours pediatrician who knew something wasn't right after going over his chart. He sent us immediately to the emergency room where a CT scan was ordered. When the doctor walked in and we saw the look on his face, we knew it was not going to be good news. When he said, "I'm sorry to tell you, your son has a brain tumor", we were in shock. His words were surreal to us. The doctor told us he had notified the neurosurgeon in the Los Angeles Kaiser Hospital and Seth was immediately taken there by ambulance. We were not allowed to ride with him as he was transported via red light and siren.

To say the least, we were in shock! We followed the ambulance down the freeway to the hospital. Seth was admitted to the Pediatric ICU and the neurosurgeon met with us to go over the surgery. He told us the tumor was in a good area and not in the brain stem. He was very optimistic about this type of surgery. Surgery was scheduled for one o'clock that day. After a five hour surgery, the good report was that the tumor was easily removed, and they felt they got it all. Seth's recovery was amazing with no other issues or complications.

Seth kept saying he wanted to go home on December 23, as he didn't want to miss Christmas. The Lord heard his prayer, and he was released from the hospital on December 23, just five days after surgery.

On January 3, Seth had a follow-up appointment with his neurosurgeon, and we were overjoyed to hear the tumor was benign and he was healing perfectly! We jumped and shouted praises and thanksgiving to Jesus, our Healer.

Seth has had several follow up MRIs and through God's grace, each time the results are always clear. Praise God for healing our son. We still maintain our prayers of faith over him and declare that "this affliction shall not rise up a second time" (Nahum 1:9).

Today Seth is a thriving, energetic boy who loves to play baseball and basketball. Out of the several baseball teams in his division, he was the only kid to hit the ball over the fence!

Chapter 22

Down Under – Another Dream Comes True

One generation should have a spiritual impact on future generations. The blessing of the Lord is destined to flow down to the children and grandchildren and on and on. The New Testament example in 2 Timothy 1:5 says: *"When I call to remembrance the unfeigned faith that is in thee, which dwelt first in thy grandmother Lois, and thy mother Eunice; and I am persuaded that in thee also."*

The Word of God, so powerful and living in the spirit and life of an individual, should spark others to walk in the ways of the Lord. This was the case in Timothy's life. His grandmother and mother made such an impact on his young life. Faith and the anointing were imparted to him through the godly training of his family. He faithfully followed the Lord and became a great pastor.

Remember Gordon's dear Aunt Mary who was used of God to bring Gordon to the knowledge of the Lord? She also had a powerful influence on her oldest son's life. Tommy Whiting was born again at a young age in Wales and followed the Lord's call into pastoral ministry. As a young man, he and his wife Violet emigrated to New Zealand to pastor in Christchurch. God used him mightily in that nation as he taught and proclaimed the Pentecostal truths. He was instrumental in the Houston family moving from New Zealand to Australia. Brian Houston, now lead pastor of Hillsong church in Sydney was only a young boy at that time.

In 1965 Gordon's cousin, Tommy, and his family moved to the Gold Coast of Australia and started a church in Southport. His two sons Stephen and Philip followed the call of God to pastor as well. His daughter, Ruth, married a pastor, and they still work in the pastoral ministry in England. There was a strong anointing on Tommy and Violet in healing, ministering the baptism in the Holy Spirit, and deliverance within the drug-infused hippie culture.

Gordon and I had contemplated going to Australia to visit his cousins, but nothing serious was planned. In 2005, we received an invitation to visit the family and minister as they were celebrating their fortieth anniversary of ministry in their church in Southport. We were delighted to be included in this grand celebration.

We spent three weeks on the Gold Coast during the month of August. It was the beginning of their spring, much like a

California winter. The whole area is beautiful, including the vast beaches.

It was such a privilege to be with family, but much more to minister to the people whose hearts were open and hungry for the Word of God. What a special family time we enjoyed together. Tommy was around ninety years old when we visited, and we sensed he would be going to heaven soon. The following year, he entered into the glory of heaven to receive his reward. We were so glad we had this special family time together.

We were so pleased to receive a visit from special friends in Australia, Ruth and Tom Nicholson. I had not seen them for many years. I had no idea Ruth would be going home to be with the Lord within a few years of our visit. On our return to California we stopped in Sydney to visit the city. It was also a joy to meet up with my longtime friend Jane Grantham. I had not seen her since 1960. We met her and her husband David at the Stamford Plaza Hotel where we were staying and enjoyed our reunion and dinner together.

While we were enjoying live piano music over dinner, Jane suddenly said, "I believe I know this musician. He is one of the Hillsong musicians."

Jane went over and spoke to him, and within a short time during a break, he joined us at our table. We knew nothing about this young man, but the Holy Spirit did. Within minutes, Gordon was ministering to him in a message in tongues. The

Lord promptly gave me the interpretation. This young man was stunned! God had read his mail and ministered directly to his heart, answering his questions and bringing hope and comfort to his situation. It was an awesome evening in the presence of the Lord! How vital it is to allow the Holy Spirit to minister as He wills wherever you are. His ministry brings life, edification, and liberty to the hearers.

We joyfully flew from Sydney back home to California with a knowing that we had followed the Holy Spirit and delivered the word of the Lord, both in the churches and in our meetings with individuals.

Chapter 23

The Now Season of My Life

> For we are God's [own] handiwork (His workmanship), recreated in Christ Jesus, [born anew] that we may do those good works which God predestined (planned beforehand) for us [taking paths which He prepared ahead of time], that we should walk in them [living the good life which He prearranged and made ready for us to live] —Ephesians 2:10 (AMP)

The life of the believer is filled with fresh, often different, and exciting seasons. The older you get the more you appreciate how God has led you perfectly through the various stages of your life. It is vital to recall how He faithfully brought you through the difficulties and challenges of life, but do not forget all the good times and abundant victories.

My life has been remarkably different since Gordon's home going. It took time and much prayer to adjust to living on my own. I knew in my heart I was not alone because Jesus never leaves or forsakes His children. My relationship with the Lord is strong, and I know who I am in Him. The part of my life that needed comfort and encouragement was in the everyday natural side of things. Living on my own and being responsible for the day-to-day living, including making decisions without the support or input of my husband, was not easy. Going out to eat by myself was another issue I had to overcome. I felt so alone and awkward when I attended any event without my husband. Driving to a new place often brought anxiety to my nervous system and emotions. Each time I asked the Holy Spirit to help me, He was always there to guide me from the simple tasks to the more difficult problems. I know that some widows are filled with shame after the death of their spouse. I must say I did not experience any shame as a result of widowhood. It did not upset me to be called a widow – I knew I was so loved by my Father God, and He was now my husband who would care for me in every way.

I was confident I should finish writing the love journey Gordon and I traveled together as husband and wife during fifty years of marriage and ministry. My journey is not complete, and my ministry tasks at this present time are moving forward as a widow, with the Lord as my husband and best friend.

I would suggest that you order and read my book, *Navigating Through the Maze of Grief.* This book documents Gordon's final season here on the earth and how I overcame the pain of loss. It will fill in some of the gaps in our story that are not included in this book. *Navigating Through the Maze of Grief* is my story of a glorious victory after loss. Everyone has suffered the loss of a loved one or friend. Facing and overcoming loss in the power of the Holy Spirit and the Word of God makes all the difference. I believe this book is anointed and will bless and encourage every reader as they face any type of loss, betrayal, or disappointment in their lives.

My deepest concern for you is that you follow and complete God's plan for your life, whether single, married, divorced, or widowed. I pray you will carefully listen to the voice of the Lord and seek Him in every decision in your life.

Gordon and I had a unique relationship in our marriage and especially in ministry. The fact that we worked together side by side for fifty years, with a heart for ministry and always desiring to fulfill God's will wherever or whatever He called us to do, was supernatural.

It could never have been accomplished without the love of God and the power and ability of the Holy Spirit. We were not perfect; we did not always see eye-to-eye on everything. But we made the decision to respect one another, even submitting to one another in the fear of the Lord (Ephesians 5:21). Gordon was my biggest fan and ministry supporter throughout our married life, and I always purposed to reciprocate in supporting him one hundred percent. Praying together daily kept us mutually glued with one purpose and heart for the preaching of the Gospel. We learned early in our marriage how to get into agreement on the Word of God and to release our faith for our provisions and receive guidance in every decision.

The example of Aquila and Pricilla in the New Testament is a blueprint for couples in ministry. When you read in the New Testament of their husband-and-wife ministry, you will understand that they were pastors and special friends of the Apostle Paul, giving him much help in his ministry (Romans 16:3; 2 Timothy 4:19). As a couple they had a pastoral and teaching ministry. They were used of God to instruct Apollos, who was eloquent in the Scriptures, but lacked knowledge of the *way of God more perfectly* (Read Acts 18: 2, 18, 26). Their instruction brought Apollos into the baptism of the Holy Spirit. Aquila and Priscilla were pastors in Corinth, having the church in their home. On three occasions in the Scriptures, Pricilla is mentioned first, quite unusual for the culture of that day.

I had a strong witness and knowing in my spirit that the Lord called me to carry on with the ministry and finish the course He had set before me. Gordon's promotion to heaven did not cancel the call of God on my life. As I waited on the Lord and prayed, instructions came little by little. It brought comfort and assurance to my soul. I knew not to rush out and do anything on my own; it was vital that I recover and heal from the natural pain of loss. God gave me wisdom in the area of making any rash changes in my life. There was plenty of time to do what God wanted me to do. Rushing into major changes, like moving, can be a big mistake. Allowing others to pressure you into doing things against what your spirit is telling you will never work out.

I also knew it was not healthy to live in isolation. I needed my family and friends in the body of Christ to support me, but at the same time I was careful not to become a clinging vine or co-dependent. My dependence was to always be on the Lord, but to also receive the warm love, support, and friendship of others. There is a balance in relationships.

Little by little I grew stronger. My heart was filled with compassion for other widows and widowers and how to minister to them. Writing was one way to accomplish this, so I started writing my book *Navigating Through the Maze of Grief*. I started a Facebook page called Winning Widows. It was an opportunity to minister to those who were processing grief, and at the same time it became a means of strength to me. The same Word I ministered to the readers became healing to my soul and emotions. Ministering to others through phone calls and emails was a channel of blessing to many. I still continue ministry to others in this way.

I keep the lines of communication open to all our friends and partners with Faith Ministries International by writing monthly newsletters. This facilitates in keeping our friends up-to-date with the activities of the ministry, including present and future plans. I know I am surrounded by the support and prayers of those who know me.

Each day with the Lord is peaceful and filled with joy and thanksgiving. I choose not to allow anything to disturb my peace. If I do permit myself to become anxious I quickly cast every care on Him and am restored to His rest in my soul. I wake up each morning with extraordinary joy accompanied with a strong purpose to do the will of the Father.

My life and calling to be a wife and helper to Gordon was a tremendous honor and then on top of that to be his partner in ministry. What glorious plans the Father has for each one of us. I truly treasure my precious memories and life as a wife and helper to my late husband.

"Having [greatly] loved His own who were in the world, He loved them [and continuously loves them with His perfect love] to the end (eternally") (John 13:1 AMP). When I read this Scripture reminding us how much Jesus loved his disciples unto the end, my heart leaped for joy as I gained further revelation into the love of God; the incredible, perfect love the Godhead has for each of us. I experienced a taste of this kind of love through my dear Gordon. He truly loved me unto the end of our days together. I honor you dear Gordon for your love and faithfulness to me.

Called to Run Our Course with Patience and Joy

> Wherefore seeing we also are compassed about with so great a cloud of witnesses, let us lay

aside every weight, and the sin which doth so easily beset us, and let us run with patience the race that is set before us. Looking unto Jesus the author and finisher of our faith; who for the joy that was set before him endured the cross, despising the shame and is set down at the right hand of the throne of God. (Hebrews 12:1-2)

Are you a runner? I know some of you love to run and compete in races. Personally, I'd rather walk. In either case, we are all called to run a spiritual race in the Kingdom of God. It is also called "walking by faith" through living, breathing, and acting on the Word of God daily. Jesus is our focus, the One who is the source and finisher of our faith, cheering us on to the finish line.

Jesus knew there would be distractions along the way, circumstances that would try to slow us down and pull us aside from running. This is why we have this admonition in Hebrews 12 to keep looking unto Jesus. Keep focused on the Word of God no matter what is trying to draw you away or scream discouragement in your ears.

God has provided two supernatural forces in our spirit that we need to stir up and one is *joy*! The other is *patience*! Joy becomes your strength, and patience keeps you constant, steady, persistent, and able to endure no matter what comes to try and hinder or stop you.

In this race we individually have our own lanes – specific callings on our lives that we are responsible to run. God has endowed us with everything we need to run, and to keep on running every day of our lives. Let your race be a delight, not a burden. Get rid of anything that would slow you down or be an encumbrance. When we understand by the Holy Spirit the will of God for our lives, we know it is exceedingly good and loaded with God's benefits on a daily basis.

The song "One In a Million" asks the question, "Why choose me, God?" Most of us have asked that question as we felt insignificant and incapable of doing what God has called us to do. But it isn't about us; it is about Jesus and the Holy Spirit and His calling, gifting, and abilities He has placed within us. When we acknowledge that "without Him we can do nothing" (John 15:5) but "with Him all things are possible" (Matthew 19:26), the anointing flows. Lean heavily on the grace and anointing of God on your life. You will be amazed what God can and will do through a yielded vessel who gives Him all the glory.

Pricilla is still here! I have purposed in my heart to keep on keeping on. I have made the decision to keep running my race every day! I'll finish my set course. In my pathway is life, and the victory has been prearranged. The finish line is guaranteed on that day when we see Jesus face to face!

Addendum

Three Years Later

The dream liner flight from London on Virgin Airlines was nearing its destination on May 26, 2017. Landing at Los Angeles meant I was close to home. This brought joy to my heart and much gratitude to the Lord for a safe and fruitful visit to England and Italy.

I have called the United States of America my home since 1969, and I am so grateful to be living in this blessed land. During a twelve year gap, from 1988 to 2000, Gordon and I lived in England, our base for our international ministry days.

After eighteen glorious days in England and Italy, memories upon memories flooded my mind and filled my heart with thanksgiving for all God had done. It all started back in January of 2017 when I felt it was the right time to return to England. It had been eight years since Gordon and I ministered together in England and other European countries. I knew there would be emotions and tears as I met with family, precious friends, and ministry colleagues. Yet in my heart I knew it would be a season of further healing from the pain and grief of loss.

I also had a knowing in my spirit that it was a pivotal season to move forward in ministry overseas. I would soon appreciate how the Lord was arranging in the spirit for future ministry in Europe.

When I returned to England in May 2017, I unexpectedly encountered grief. I should have known this was not unusual. It would hit me suddenly when I met pastors, ministers, family, and friends. I thought of all the times Gordon and I had ministered together in this land. Reality hit me when he was no longer by my side as before. Grief hit me with a force. I immediately turned to the Holy Spirit to help me process it and release the hidden sadness. As quickly as I could, I acknowledged its presence, then let it go and received sweet healing in my emotions.

I thought before I left home that grief was completely gone but when it reared its ugly head I knew by the Spirit what to do—face it and recognize it for what it is, and allow His grace to minister to me. His grace was more than sufficient, and healing came. I trust this encourages you and other widows' hearts and emotions to know the Holy Spirit continues to heal the deepest recesses of our soul with His Word and by the power of the Holy Spirit.

My assistant Mary Venanzi accompanied me from California. For our stay in England, a sweet reunion ensued on

Addendum

our arrival in Haselmere, Surrey, as longtime minister friend Mieke Colleé hosted us. Her loving British and European hospitality refreshed us each day of our stay.

Spring is such a colorful time of year in England. The azaleas, rhododendrons, and other gorgeous flowering trees and spring flowers were in full bloom, standing out in vivid contrast to the varied green hues of the grassy fields and shrubs. We glimpsed only a few remaining patches of blue bells as they had bountifully flowered earlier in the month. Long time friend Marian Cox drove us around the Surrey hills and countryside on winding roads to local gardens and tea shops.

A day trip to London's Waterloo station by train brought further memories to light. Barb Witt was our guide on this lovely sunny day, in the high 60s, with a nice breeze. After a short bus ride from the station, we disembarked and walked across Westminster Bridge, past the Houses of Parliament towards Westminster Abbey and Parliament Square. A walk up Whitehall Street past Downing Street and the changing of the guards brought us to Trafalgar Square. Memories flooded my mind as I visualized when Gordon preached and sang at the base of Nelson's Column between the giant lions. The London Revival Crusade held an evangelist outreach there during the Whitsun (Pentecost) holiday weekend in May of 1964.

The next step was to search for the Orange Street Congregational Church, located on a narrow street sandwiched between the National Art Gallery and Leicester Square. This church was founded by the Huguenots who escaped from France in the 1600s. At one time, the church's pastor was Rev. Augustus Toplady, who wrote the famous hymn, "Rock of Ages." Gordon and I ministered to the hippie generation in the 1960s with an outreach in Leicester Square and the Soho district. After preaching on the streets with others from the London Revival Crusade, the young people were invited to the basement of Orange Street church for tea and biscuits and presented with the Gospel. I felt such nostalgia as I envisioned those early days of our ministry in London. In our wildest dreams, we never thought this was but the beginning of a ministry that spanned fifty years to the nations.

Next door to the church, a plaque is displayed on a newer building honoring Sir Isaac Newton, whose home at one time was next to the Orange Street Church, and where he attended from time to time.

We boarded a bus to St. Paul's Cathedral, London Bridge, and Tower Bridge. Again I thought of the time I had worked in the old city of London not far from this well-known historic area. On our return to catch our train home, we passed through Fleet Street and the Strand where I once worked for a solicitor whose office was located opposite the Law Courts.

I was the guest speaker for Pastor Jim Patterson of Wellspring Pentecostal Church in Welling, Kent, on Sunday May 14, an Assemblies of God church with people hungry for the things of the Spirit.

Addendum

The following is a report from Pastor Jim,

> A young deacon at Wellspring, who you met and prayed with to receive the baptism in the Holy Spirit, had mentioned to me how when you prayed for him, he burst into speaking and singing in the Spirit. Two days later, he was booked to speak at our Bible study and prayer meeting, and while we were in a short time of worship, he began to speak clearly and loudly in the language of the Spirit. After that, he gave a very powerful message. He shared how that when he heard you were coming to minister in Wellspring and that God had given you a prophetic ministry, he believed that when you would pray for him, he would be filled with the Holy Spirit. To God be all the glory.

Barb Witt's Ministry

On Saturday May 20, I ministered for Barb Witt Ministries at the Holiday Inn in Guildford, Surrey. It was a joy to reconnect with Barb. She had faithfully served Gordon and I in our ministry during the 1990s in both London and Guildford. Today Barb is an ordained minister under Faith Ministries

International, flowing in the anointing of a teacher in the Body of Christ. She is an author of faith-building teaching books.

The people drew from the Word of God and the anointing as I ministered. The prophetic flowed and I ministered to the sick.

I reconnected with those who had been blessed under our ministry over the years. One such couple was James and Bola Ashaye from London. I was so happy to see the Ashaye's son, Joshua, a brilliant, tall young man who is preparing to be a doctor. The Ashaye's testimony of miracle children is included in this book.

Ministry in Italy

As the plane landed in Pescara on the Adriatic I think my heart skipped a few beats with the joy of being reunited to Maria Rossi Di Francesco. I had not seen Maria since 2003. We had met in Belgium in 1991, when she was our interpreter at a church outside Brussels. Maria worked for us in Faith Ministries International in England for a number of years, often interpreting for us into the French language. She translated Gordon's book into French, *What on Earth Are You Saying?* many years ago. This book is still distributed in French-speaking nations.

Maria, now married to Mario, the Lord has blessed them with two beautiful children, Paolo and Gloria. They welcomed us into their lovely home and showered us with warm

Italian hospitality. Maria is an anointed woman of God, who is ordained under the ministry. I was invited to share the Word of God on the Tuesday evening to the home group from her church. The teaching on compassion and the ministry of reconciliation flowed with an encouraging prophetic word for the believers. Maria interpreted for me, and there was a beautiful flow in the spirit, reminding me of years gone by when we had ministered together in many meetings.

Ministering in Italy was a first for me, and I believe it is not the last! Europe is very much in my heart, a dry and thirsty part of the world that needs to hear the Gospel and see the gracious manifestations of the Holy Spirit.

The Journey Goes On

At the time of the publication of this book, the "love journey" with Jesus goes on. The passion and love of God poured out in my heart by the Holy Spirit propels me to reach the unreached and teach the untaught the glorious Truth of God's unchanging Word.

Wise words to those who are beginning their journey in ministry. Stay humble and committed to follow the Lord's plan for your life. Remain steadfast and unmovable as the Holy Spirit instructs you in the way you should go.

About The Author

Barbara J White is based in Southern California, where she conducts Faith Ministries International, an evangelistic, teaching, prophetic, and healing ministry.

Barbara has many years of experience in the pastoral and traveling ministry to the nations. She has also ministered for women's conferences in the United States and hosted Faith Women International conferences in Amsterdam, Brussels, London; as well as in Bermuda. Barbara follows the call of God on her life from early childhood.

For over fifty years, she and her husband, Gordon, traveled and ministered together on six continents. Their anointed husband-and-wife ministry began in the United Kingdom, followed by ministry in the United States and then to the nations. Throughout their pastoral and international ministry, the Lord was pleased to confirm His word through many signs and wonders. By the anointing of the Holy Spirit, miracles, healing gifts, and prophetic utterances have followed the preaching and teaching of God's Word.

Barbara's loving husband, Gordon White, was promoted to heaven on June 26, 2014. She continues to follow God's plan for her life, teaching faith, healing, and motivating the body of Christ to live in victory. Her ministry flows in the anointing with manifestations of the gifts of the Holy Spirit.

Resources

Barbara is the author of *Navigating Through the Maze of Grief*, *Say the Word*, *Job's Jeopardy*, and many mini-teaching books to build your faith in the integrity of God's Word.

Winning Widows is a group page on Facebook, devoted to ministering to the emotional support and spiritual needs of widows and those who have lost loved ones. You are invited to join to receive daily inspirational Bible devotions.

Faith Ministries International: Barbara's ministry page is available on Facebook. When you join you will receive monthly teaching newsletters and ministry updates.

Barbara is available to speak to your church, group, or teaching seminar.
www.fmint.org

CPSIA information can be obtained
at www.ICGtesting.com
Printed in the USA
FSHW02n1027020518
47700FS